2. New loans should be halted to governments where the world community has achieved broad consensus as to their blatant disregard for development and the basic needs of the majority. South Africa would be at the top of this list.

Medium-term Measures

3. For the remaining debtor nations, new International Monetary Fund (IMF) programs should replace the traditional austerity measures with an emphasis on development programs that create jobs; advance health, housing, education, and other basic needs; narrow the gap between rich and poor; and manage natural resources for sustainable development.

4. A debt-relief program should be initiated that converts portions of Third World debt into grants; extends periods for repaying the remaining debt; and sets a ceiling on debt service as a share of a country's export earnings at 20 percent.

5. U.S. bilateral aid should be overhauled to channel more aid to institutions that encourage self-reliance and involvement of the poor. Military and security-related aid should be cut and replaced with greater development assistance.

6. Government regulation of banks should be directed toward preventing future massive and unchecked overseas lending. Mechanisms should also be created to insure more meaningful public regulation of banks bailed out by the U.S. government.

Long-term Measures

7. A reformed and democratized IMF should be reduced to coordinating foreign exchange policies of its members and responding to their truly short-term financing needs.

Other Policies

8. U.S. federal budget deficits should be reduced by cutting military spending and restoring corporate taxes. With the deficit reduction, the United States could more easily reduce interest rates whose high levels have added billions of dollars to developing countries' debt service payments.

9. A managed trade system, integrated with a national industrial policy, is needed to preserve and modernize selected U.S. industries and provide adequate job retraining for workers in dying industries. Tax and tariff policies that encourage corporations to move production offshore should be eliminated.

10. The domestic farm crisis should be met with a sound agriculture policy that reverses growing control of non-producers over producers, and guarantees debt relief for family farmers, an equitable policy of world food security, a system of resource conservation, and a sound domestic food assistance policy.

From DEBT To DEVELOPMENT

Alternatives to the International Debt Crisis

A Working Group of
THE DEBT CRISIS NETWORK

Published by the Institute for
Policy Studies

Copies of this book are available
from the Institute for Policy Studies, 1901 Q Street, NW, Washington, DC 20009.

ISBN 0 89758 041 9

A Working Group of
THE DEBT CRISIS NETWORK

John Cavanagh
IPS

Fantu Cheru
Development GAP

Carole Collins
IPS

Cameron Duncan
American University

Dominic Ntube
Bread for the World

CONTENTS

PREFACE

Over the past five years, the world economy has been mired in its gravest postwar crisis. Glimpses of its effects are seen in graphic photos of famine in Africa, riots in the Dominican Republic, rainforest destruction in Brazil, and unemployment lines in England.

At the center of this crisis stands a burden that threatens the stability of the entire system: almost $900 billion in Third World debt owed to western banks and governments. These banks and governments have responded to the debt build-up in a fashion destructive of democracy and development. They have imposed austerity on, and are draining capital out of, the Third World.

These deteriorating conditions for the world's majority should be among the list of Americans' priorities for action. Economic shortages and austerity are the greatest threat to democracy and stability in the Third World today. When the President speaks of the threat to national security in Central America, he should be speaking of the grinding poverty, the environmental destruction, and the collapse of finance, trade and production. As these conditions worsen, U.S. jobs and communities and real security also suffer.

Concerned about these trends, representatives of religious organizations, unions, environmental groups, hunger and development organizations, researchers, and other citizens groups gathered in September of 1984 to address the international debt crisis. United around a commitment to social justice and to more just, equitable and long-term solutions to the debt crisis, they launched a Debt Crisis Network in April of 1985. A special working group was established to write a report to demystify the debt crisis, and answer certain fundamental questions. Who does it affect? Where did it come from? Is it, as some bankers have argued, over? What solutions might ease the burden of debt and bring the Third World closer to participatory development?

For far too long, debate on the international debt crisis has been monopolized by the few. It is no surprise that the very

2

bankers and government officials responsible for building up the debt are the same ones who dominate discussions about solutions. The poor and working majorities of the world, on whose shoulders the brunt of the crisis has been placed, have almost no voice in the current debate.

Ultimately, pressure for more humane policy toward the rest of the world must come from a far better informed public. This book is written to inform, and to stimulate debate from church parishes to union halls, from city councils to high school classrooms.

For editorial and other assistance, we thank: Nancy Alexander, Carol Barr, Carol Barton, Shantilal Bhagat, Robert Borosage, Patricia Brady, Barbara Bramble, Robin Broad, Robert Browne, Chat Canlas, Frederick Clairmonte, Fred Cook, Tom Fues, Guy Gran, Richard Grossman, Doug Hellinger, Judy Hurley, Marina Lent, Isabel Letelier, Arjun Makhijani, Michael McCoy, Martin McLaughlin, Cynthia Obadia, Cheryl Payer, Lee Price, Pat Rumer, Audrey Smock, Jorge Sol, Ludger Volmer, David Ward, Al Watkins, Barbara Weaver, Barbara Wien, David Williams and Kelly Yencer.

Martha Doggett performed a tremendous job of copy editing the work. Many at the Institute for Policy Studies helped in seeing the manuscript through from start to finish. We also extend thanks to Mark Decker for typesetting the manuscript.

Finally, we gratefully acknowledge grants from the Women's Division of the United Methodist General Board of Global Ministries and the United Church Board for World Ministries that made the production of this work possible.

Debt Crisis Network Coordinating Committee

John Cavanagh
Institute for Policy Studies

Cynthia Obadia
Quaker UN Office

Dominic Ntube
Bread for the World

David Williams
Council on Hemispheric Affairs

Barbara Weaver
Women's Division, United Methodist Board of Global Ministries

Barbara Wien
World Policy Institute

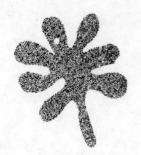

I

Introduction

The Setting

Over the past half decade, the living standards of the vast majority of the 2.5 billion people in the Third World have deteriorated sharply. Most families are receiving less real income that must pay for more costly goods. Disease and malnutrition have spread. Prospects for reversal are bleak as billions more dollars flow out of the developing world yearly than come in.

Living standards for the majority in the developed world, while much higher, likewise suffered in the face of rising unemployment, economic stagnation, and high interest rates.

At the center of this deterioration lies a crisis of almost unprecedented global proportions. In 1984, the Third World owed Western banks and governments $895 billion, a sum equivalent to the vast amounts spent on armaments worldwide each year.[1] While measurable in dollars, the crisis takes its toll on human beings with a brutality that is difficult to capture in words.

- A grocery shopper in Santo Domingo finds cooking oil prices doubled overnight as part of an International Monetary Fund (IMF) package.
- A bus driver greets a worker in Manila with a 30 percent fare increase necessary to cover petroleum price hikes that were part of a similar package.
- A peasant in the Northeast of Brazil learns that farm credit to pay for essential fertilizer is no longer available, axed in the latest IMF agreement.

- Hundreds of small businessmen close shop in Santiago, unable to compete as tariffs and other protections are eliminated as a result of an IMF agreement.
- The incidence of disastrous oil leaks and industrial accidents escalates in Mexico as the oil industry is set on a breakneck growth path in order to meet the country's debt payments.
- U.S. workers in export-oriented industries are laid off by the hundreds of thousands as Third World countries—following IMF advice—slash imports in an attempt to eliminate trade deficits.
- U.S. taxpayers unwittingly take over Continental Illinois through a federal bailout, though the "new owners" are given absolutely no say over its operations.

The relationships between these events and these individuals are hidden from most of us; even the victims rarely get explanations. International debt is often presented as a problem for large banks and governments that is being resolved among them. The impact of their "resolutions" on workers, peasants, farmers, the environment, and the entire process of development is presented separately, in bits and pieces, and seldom from the viewpoint of the victims. Too often, the debt crisis is viewed only as affecting profligate Third World countries and their peoples. Too seldom are the real costs borne by workers and other citizens in the United States and Europe added to the equation.

The crisis affects all of us. If left to the board rooms of banks and finance ministries, the worker, the farmer, the entrepreneur, and the poor will bear the costs of the extravagant mistakes of the powerful. This report is based on the premise that only an informed citizenry can act to insure that the problem's roots are addressed equitably. To aid in this process, the report spells out what the debt crisis is, who it affects, where it came from, and what solutions might move the world a step closer from debt toward development.

As an introduction, this chapter assesses the geographic spread of international debt and the specific impact of debt on different segments of the developing world. It concludes with an overview of the increasingly adverse impact of the crisis on the United States, and the urgency of reform.

Magnitude of the Debt Crisis

Third World debt has spiralled over the last decade as a result of careless and aggressive lending practices by transnational banks and ill-conceived growth strategies in many developing countries. In order to pay interest on their enormous debts, developing countries have been pressured by the world's economic policeman—the IMF—to cut domestic spending, end food subsidies, freeze wages, and cheapen ("devalue") currencies. The poor and middle classes have borne the brunt of these measures. If a date had to be placed on when the rising debt spiral became a crisis for the world economy as a whole, it would be the infamous "Mexican weekend" of August 1982, when the Mexican government publicized its inability to service the country's $80 billion debt. Sixteen months later, by the end of 1983, 42 countries were behind in the debt payments.[2]

Across the Third World, the burden of debt has not been equally distributed. It is useful to distinguish three categories of developing countries for whom the debt crisis has left different imprints: the big seven, small debtors with large burdens, and the world's poorest nations.

Seven countries alone account for almost half of the $895 billion total Third World debt: Brazil, Mexico, Argentina, and Venezuela in Latin America; and South Korea, the Philippines, and Indonesia in Asia. With debt burdens surpassing $25 billion each, these seven constitute the biggest worry for the large banks.[3] The default of one of these countries would shake the entire international financial system; their collective default could bring it down.

A second group of debtors includes around 40-50 countries with debts that are large in proportion to their domestic capacity to repay, but not large enough to precipitate world financial crisis. These include about two dozen African countries for whom the debt crisis is now exacerbating hunger and malnutrition, as well as countries such as Bolivia, Peru, Ecuador, and Chile. They also include the five Central American nations ravaged by political crisis and war—Costa Rica, El Salvador, Guatemala, Honduras, and Nicaragua. While debt as a proportion of gross national product averaged 36 percent for all of Latin America in 1983, it averaged 71 percent for these five nations.[4] Most of these countries lack the democratic political structures and economies that are a prerequisite to authentic development. Few possess the industrial and agricultural infrastructure necessary to expand production and exports, or to pay off debts and begin the development process.

There is a third group of Third World countries that are not significant debtors by any measure (international significance or debt-bearing capacity), but that are nevertheless seriously affected by the operation of the international financial system. These countries do not have large debts because they have been regarded as poor credit risks by banks. This third group covers much of the Third World, including its very poorest countries.

Effects in the Developing World

Analytically, it is useful to distinguish three distinct mechanisms through which the debt crisis affects Third World populations:

Export-led growth

Countries mired in debt surrender a portion of their sovereignty in setting economic policy to the IMF, the World Bank, and other external institutions. The prevailing wisdom in these institutions—the same wisdom that spurred many of the countries to borrow so much in the first place—is that export-led growth with minimal government interference in the market is the best course to follow. Certainly this path has benefitted some in the export sector. But, it also has led to malnutrition and suffering for others. In countries with limited resources, the spread of export crops often usurps land once devoted to staple food crops. Peasants are dislocated from rural areas to urban slums to make way for export plantations. Formal jobs in the cities are few; poverty and malnutrition are often rampant.

Financial crunch

After two decades of abundant lending, private banks have cut back new loans substantially in the past four years. One set of figures illustrates the effects: in 1983, $50 billion flowed out of developing countries to service debt payments. The same countries received only $20 billion in private bank loans and another $15 billion from multilateral financial institutions. Without considering the tens of billions of dollars in capital fleeing developing countries, a net outflow of $15 billion was drained from the Third World that year.[5] Banks also continue to demand repayment of some of the interest on past loans. The result is a severe shortage of foreign exchange in many developing countries.

IMF austerity

In most Third World discussions of the impact of the debt crisis, IMF austerity or conditionality is mentioned first. The IMF lends to a financially troubled country only after that country submits to an economic program of "demand management." The logic behind the program is that if a country is spending more than it takes in, demand for goods and services must be reduced, imports cut, and exports boosted.

This is traditionally done through a combination of policies: making imports more expensive (via devaluation of the currency), making basic goods more expensive (via the elimination of government subsidies), and freezing the real wages of workers. Government expenditures are also reduced by cutting out social welfare programs and cutting subsidized credits to farmers.

The treatment might be summarized as follows: the IMF approaches its patient in much the same fashion as the medieval doctor. Regardless of the disorder, leeches are applied and the patient is bled. At best, the remedy supplants the original disorder with a new agony, often more lethal than the original. Even for countries where the IMF "remedy" ups the trade balance, the underlying debt and development crises go on, and the pain produced is severe.

Different segments of Third World populations respond to the bleeding, the financial squeeze, and the export orientation in different ways.

The *rural poor, peasantry, and small farmers* have been widely affected by the zeal with which export-led development models have been pursued at a moment in history when world trade has stagnated. The volume of world trade simply did not grow in the four years from 1980 through 1983, and the effect of dozens of developing countries attempting to flood export markets with their coffee, cocoa, clothing, coconuts and copper has been to drive down the prices of these products.[6] Among the results: world sugar prices hovered around 5-6 cents/pound in early 1985, while production costs in the Philippines, for example, stood at 12-14 cents/pound.[7]

Insistence in IMF programs that the government cut subsidized credits to farmers has at times led to severe shortages of pesticides, fertilizers, and other essential agricultural inputs for debt-ridden, small farmers. In Zambia, for example, a 1978 IMF-advised cutback in rural credits led to a precipitous drop in maize production and an increase in malnutrition.[8] Today, in Africa, such measures have combined with the worst drought in the last century to dispossess millions of agricultural producers in over two dozen countries. IMF officials are often quick to point out that one of their favored policy recommendations can benefit the rural sector, namely lifting government controls that have kept urban prices of many agricultural products quite low. While partially true, the assertion ignores the fact that such resulting price increases are seldom passed on to agricultural workers on fixed salaries, and are devastating to the urban poor.

The *urban poor*, including unemployed and marginally employed populations, are especially vulnerable to such pricing policy changes. Many have incomes that are unstable or fixed at very low levels. Overnight doubling or tripling of bean, rice, tortilla, or cooking oil prices can follow the signing of an IMF agreement, often sparking what is popularly viewed as an IMF institution: a food riot. The currency devaluations that are part of IMF agreements push up import prices and, in turn, stimulate the general inflation rate. After three devaluations over a 13-month period (1983-1984), the Philippines' poorest urban families paid 80 percent more for the same basket of groceries.[9]

IMF agreements also counsel the cutback of government expenditures in other areas, including public employment programs, and social and public servies. The urban poor are particularly dependent on such programs.

Women make up the majority of the Third World rural (and particularly rural poor) population. They produce the bulk of food in developing countries and, for example, make up 60-80 percent of the agricultural workforce in Africa.[10] Hence, labor-displacing shifts from food to export crops hit women the hardest.

Famine, debt, and regional conflicts throughout the Third World have produced nearly constant flows of refugees desperately searching for food and water; over 75 percent of the world's refugees are women and children. The Sudan alone is currently trying to handle two million refugees; six million of its own people are facing famine.

Sex discrimination has left women with fewer economic resources to weather stiff austerity plans. Fewer opportunities for wage employment are open to women, who also suffer lower wage levels, more layoffs and prohibitions in some countries against owning land. Likewise, women usually have less access to basic education, health care, clean water, and agricultural services, and are therefore especially hard hit by austerity measures that cut government spending in these areas.

Despite the weight of the crisis that is shouldered by women, they play only a minimal role in decision-making in the institutions that advocate and administer austerity both nationally and internationally.

Another particularly vulnerable group in the Third World is *children*. Debt has stimulated a deterioration in nutritional and health standards in recent years, with concomitant rising infant mortality. The problem has reached staggering proportions in Sub-Saharan Africa where, in 1980, 44 percent of the estimated population consisted of children under 15 years of age. This translates into 92 dependents for every 100 active persons. In the absence of formal public or private social security, this politically unrepresented grouping quietly suffers much of the burden of economic austerity.

Urban workers are affected by most of the same factors that erode the economic sustenance of the urban poor. In addition, IMF stabilization programs also generally involve a freeze in workers' real wages. This proves a very difficult policy to implement with precision or equity in countries with high inflation rates. While prices rise daily or weekly, wages are usually indexed upward only a couple times per year. In countries where prices rise more than 100 percent annually (not a rare occurrence in Latin America), workers start losing purchasing power the day after each wage adjustment.[11]

Workers suffer from IMF medicine in yet another fashion. The one area of debt-ridden economies where the IMF has advocated growth—export-oriented agriculture and industry—is precisely the area least protected by labor law in most countries. Most Third World industrialization geared for export takes place in free trade zones devoid of any guarantees of internationally recognized labor standards.[12] Typically the guarantees run in the other direction: transnational corporations in the zone are promised that workers will not strike, unionize, etc. In some cases, the IMF has also pushed the dismantling of labor laws. In 1984, the IMF requested that laws protecting workers from arbitrary dismissal in Peru be repealed.[13]

A final social class adversely affected by current remedies to the debt crisis is *domestic entrepreneurs*. Many entrepreneurs producing for domestic markets have gone bankrupt as policy incentives are shifted to favor exporters. The elimination of protective tariffs and the difficulty in obtaining foreign exchange for vital raw material and machinery imports have accelerated the liquidation of small- and medium-sized enterprises. In the process, tens of thousands are thrown out of work. Capital and machinery are underutilized and the country is that much farther from repaying its debts.

One other victim of debt crisis management in the Third World, affecting virtually everyone, is the *environment*. As governments of developing countries adopt austerity measures, cuts in social services are often accompanied by the dismantling of state environmental controls and programs to control soil erosion, over-intensive cropping, desertification, and resource depletion. These cuts occur when the programs are needed most: as the social classes hit by the crisis scramble to stretch land and resources to their limit.

As governments attempt to step up export activities, expansion often occurs in pesticide and fertilizer-intensive agriculture, adding to the thousands of pesticide-related deaths that yearly plague the Third World.[14] Mineral and petroleum extraction is invariably sped up, leading to such disasters as the

1979 Mexican oil spill, the worst spill in Latin American history.

Beyond the specific impacts of the debt crisis looms the larger, overall question of development. In the IMF's quest for short-term, stop-gap remedies to trade and payments imbalances, it has ignored the longer-term consequences of its programs. In turn, much of the debate in financial circles has revolved around how to save the banks and how to insure that Argentina and Brazil meet their next repayment deadline. Certain ominous trends from within the Third World have been all but ignored.

As government spending has been cut and as most available foreign exchange has been spent servicing debt in many countries, programs vital to development have been neglected. New investment projects in agriculture have been halted in many African countries. Roads, dams, utilities, and other basic infrastructure has been neglected. Industry in more advanced developing countries has decayed from lack of essential raw materials and spare parts, leading to deindustrialization that will take years, if not decades, to reverse. Carefully built linkages between producers and their indigenous suppliers that are so vital to independent development have crumbled.

In brief, a review of the past three years will reveal that dozens of Third World countries have, under IMF tutelage, improved their short-term trade positions, but few have gained in any of the indicators that measure real, sustainable development. Rather, most have slid backward amidst growing inequity, environmental degradation, deindustrialization, and poverty. This is the most important challenge in addressing the debt crisis—the challenge of dealing with the crisis in a manner that stimulates development.

Effects in the United States

Does the impact of the debt crisis stop at the southern banks of the Rio Grande, the shores of the Mediterranean, and the upper reaches of Southeast Asia? According to the financial press of the Western world, by and large the answer is yes. They report banks are resilient, our economies will rebound, and the Third World will be pulled back on its feet.

Voices articulating another answer to that question are, however, beginning to be heard. They come from union halls, farmer alliances, concerned taxpayers, and even small banks. When pieced together, they tell quite a different story.

Thus far, *workers in export-oriented industries* have borne the brunt of the crisis. Since the heart of IMF adjustment is a substantial contraction of imports and since about a third of U.S. trade is with the Third World, the consequences are quite predictable: massive job loss in certain U.S. industries.

Estimates of job cutbacks due to the debt crisis vary widely. Gerard Adams of Wharton Economic Forecasting Associates testified before the Joint Economic Committee of Congress in June 1985 that the United States had lost 800,000 jobs as a result of the debt crisis in Latin America alone.[15] Another estimate sets the decline in jobs caused by the drop in exports to the Third World between 1980 and 1983 (due to debt and other causes) at 1.1 million.[16] The United Auto Workers has estimated that the U.S. manufacturing trade balance plummeted from a $17 billion surplus in 1980 to an $80 billion deficit in 1984. Using the Commerce Department's estimate that $1 billion in trade creates 25,000 jobs, around 2.4 million jobs were lost due to trade shifts. While it is difficult to determine how many of these jobs were lost as a direct result of debt-induced IMF austerity, debt is certainly the leading single cause of the decline.

Agriculture and capital goods jobs have suffered the worst. Farming has become highly dependent on exports over the last two decades, and the weakening of foreign markets has deepened the worst agricultural slump in the United States since the Depression. Likewise, employment in farm equipment, construction machinery, civilian aircraft, and other capital goods industries dependent on exports has fallen 20-50 percent in the last few years. All of these job losses create harmful ripple effects in surrounding communities.

Declining export markets are not the only way in which Third World debt has affected *U.S. farmers*. The flip side of IMF policies to reduce Third World imports has been efforts to boost Third World exports, the largest category of which remain agricultural commodities. Some of these, such as corn, rice, and soybeans, compete directly with U.S. output and the flooding of world markets drives down world prices, undermining the position of farmers everywhere.

Farmers are not only affected by Third World debt; they are undergoing a debt crisis of remarkably similar magnitude. In 1970, U.S. farm debt stood at $35 billion; it rose to $166 billion a decade later. By year end 1984, it reached $215 billion (greater than the combined debt of Brazil and Mexico) and the upward trend has continued.[17] Both U.S. farmers and the Third World have fallen victim to, and exercise no control over, high and fluctuating interest rates generated by U.S. budget deficits and Federal Reserve Board monetary policies. Finally, both are "price-takers," not "price-makers," of the commodities they produce and have faced prices in recent years that no longer cover basic costs of production.

Exacerbated by land speculation, the farm debt crisis has dealt a wrenching social blow not only to farmers, but also to local banks, stores, sharecroppers, and rural children. Among those most seriously affected are medium-sized family farmers. In both 1982 and 1983, 20,000 farmers went out of business. As many as 80,000 farms are estimated to have gone under in 1984.[18] According to the U.S. Department of Agriculture: "Among the 679,000 family sized commercial farms on January 1, 1985, 229,000 farms, owing over forty-six percent of all farm debt, had financial problems ranging from difficulty servicing debts to technical insolvency."[19]

Nearly a third of farmers borrowing from the Farmers' Home Administration (FmHA) are delinquent in repaying their loans.[20] Since income into rural America—for retail purchases, bank deposits, local taxes, churches—enters primarily through local farmer income, the debt crisis has contributed to a contraction in retailing, farm equipment and input industries, and an eroding tax base from which public and social services are funded.

Taxpayers are only now glimpsing the magnitude of costs they will be expected to cover. As overexposed banks begin to fail, U.S. citizens will increasingly be asked to pick up the tab for unregulated overseas lending by U.S. banks. The Continental Illinois bailout, partially related to Third World lending, cost American taxpayers approximately $4.5 billion, around $20 per person. Rising numbers of *small banks* have also been edged into bankruptcy, in part due to their participation in loans syndicated by larger banks on which developing countries have suspended repayment. How patient will American taxpayers be in bailing out U.S. banks that have increasingly served the financing needs of American multinationals while depriving communities of desperately needed loans?

The Urgency of Reform

Thus far, the crisis has been managed by transnational banks and the IMF in a piecemeal, country-by-country approach. While forestalling the collapse of the entire financial system, this management has been anti-development, destabilizing and inequitable in a fashion that will have serious long-term consequences.

In addition to the daily human suffering generated by current methods, the erosion of infrastructure and industry in several of the more advanced developing countries will be difficult to reverse. The slashing of vital raw material and capital goods imports in Brazil, the Philippines, and elsewhere (as these countries try to achieve IMF-decreed trade surpluses) has crippled existing industrial capacity.

To insure that debt service payments continue in the absence of new credit, Third World countries have cut imports by almost half.[21] Under IMF austerity guidelines, imports have been cut by reducing demand, usually by devaluing the local currency. As the tide of international credit has shifted from an inflow to an outflow, far less credit remains for internal use in Third World countries. Not only are many private sector borrowers squeezed, but government spending has been slashed.

In terms of stability, the poorer majorities in more and more developing countries are no longer remaining silent in the face of IMF austerity. Over the past two years, food riots have rocked Brazil, the Sudan, and the Dominican Republic. Millions have poured into the streets of Chile and the Philippines challenging the legitimacy of regimes that starve their own people. If political instability in the Southern Hemisphere is a major threat to U.S. national security, then the debt crisis and the failure of development, not East-West conflict, is the major culprit. As poverty and popular unrest in the Third World grow, peace everywhere is placed in danger.

The debt crisis—and current IMF policies supposedly aimed at its alleviation—have also eroded the economic stability of developed countries' economies and banking systems. In turn, it has affected not only Third World but also U.S. farmers, businesses, workers, taxpayers, and the poor. The social and economic costs of repayment of world debt have been pushed onto those most vulnerable to, yet least responsible for, the crisis. The urgency for change could not be greater.

II

Origins of the Crisis

Introduction

A popular rendition of the debt crisis has been widely publicized in the financial press and by the major television networks over the past couple of years. It is popular because it is simple, optimistic, and stops short of assessing blame. This chapter begins with that version and ends with another: one which examines the structural and institutional roots of debt and underdevelopment. By understanding the historic role and responsibility of the various actors, one can begin to sketch effective policies to move from debt to development.

Despite several variants, the popular version of the debt crisis revolves around four dates: 1973 (the origin), 1979, 1982, and 1984 (marking the crisis-end):

1973

The Organization of Petroleum Exporting Countries (OPEC) quadruples oil prices virtually overnight and floods the Western banking system with billions of dollars. The banks, in turn, lend most of the new inflow to developing countries eager to grow rapidly.

1979

OPEC sets off a second quadrupling of oil prices at a time when some of the earlier developing country debts fall due. At the same time, as a result of the U.S. federal deficit and tight monetary policy, U.S. interest rates begin to soar. Saddled with enormously high oil import and debt service bills, certain developing economies begin to look shaky. Their new borrowing is eaten up almost entirely by paying these two bills.

1982

Panic seizes the world financial community as the largest debtors dramatically announce their inability to continue servicing their enormous debts. The trigger date of the crisis is a weekend in August 1982 (dubbed "The Mexican Weekend" in financial circles) when Mexican officials tell the U.S. Treasury Department they can't meet payments to commercial banks on their $80 billion external debt. Brazil, Argentina, Venezuela, and the Philippines follow with similar announcements. Two years of frantic, patchwork deals follow, where the IMF hammers out dozens of standby arrangements, jumbo loans, and so-called "rescue" packages to tide over desperate debtors.

1984

In August 1984, commercial bank and government officials iron out a unique solution with Mexico (dubbed "the Mexico deal") whereby Mexico accepts a new austerity program, agrees to continue interest payments, but gets most of its debt rescheduled and a 14-year reprieve before it must resume principal payments. This establishes a model for other large debtors and, before year-end, the IMF and commercial banks achieve new agreements with the other four major problem debtors: Brazil, Venezuela, the Philippines, and Argentina. Bankers proclaim that the debt crisis is over, after nine years in the making, two years of boiling, and several months of clever management.

Blame, in this version, is seldom assessed. The major culprit is external shocks, primarily induced by 13 large oil exporting nations. The key countries are Mexico, Argentina, Brazil, Venezuela, the Philippines, and the United States. Africa, Central America, other parts of Latin America do not exist. Victims of the crisis in the Third World are faceless. Development is not at issue. Banks did what they were supposed to do—recycle money. And, at the crucial moment, the IMF and the U.S. Treasury Department rose to the task and patched it all up. End of story.

Another version of the debt crisis begins much earlier in time. It examines the structural inequities built into the current international financial order, as well as the nondemocratic nature of politics and economics in much of the world. It studies the role played by the four key sets of actors in the crisis: private transnational banks and corporations; developing country governments; developed country governments; and the multilateral agencies, particularly the IMF and the World Bank. It assesses unforeseen shocks to the system, such as oil price increases and African drought, as symptoms of a deeper systemic crisis. Finally, it examines how growth models in underdeveloped countries exacerbated inequalities and induced debt which, in turn, induced further underdevelopment. No simple causes. No easy answers.

Structural Roots of the Crisis

Large-scale borrowing and dependent forms of Third World growth were virtually built into the postwar international economic system sketched out in 1944 by the United States and its allies at Bretton Woods, New Hampshire. Borrowing and dependency were encouraged both by the new institutions set up to govern the international economy, and by the continuation of an international division of labor between developed and developing countries that had roots stretching far back into the history of colonialism.

The colonial division of labor was based on the unequal exchange of manufactured goods from the industrializing metropoles for agricultural and mineral raw materials from the colonies, or periphery. From the outset, the prices of the raw materials both fluctuated more wildly and tended to rise more slowly than those of manufactured commodities. This made planning difficult in the periphery, and was one key factor that created an incentive for borrowing. Rather than addressing this fundamental imbalance, governments and business interests in the metropoles responded by expanding institutions that lent— transnational commercial banks, and later by creating the IMF and multilateral development banks.

Rapid price fluctuations of raw commodities derive from several factors. Agricultural raw materials are prone to the vagaries of nature: frost, flood, drought, fire, etc. Prices can shift quickly as demand for these products grows or shrinks in the developed world. The decision by Coca Cola and other soft drink manufacturers to replace sugar with corn-based and then artificial sweetners, for example, contributed to send sugar prices to historic lows in 1984 and 1985. In the two decades following World War II, the World Bank and IMF estimated that fluctuations in export prices were two and a half to three times greater in developing countries than in developed countries.[1]

Declining terms of trade for developing countries—the phenomenon of export prices rising slower than prices of imported manufactures—was first observed by the United Nations Economic Commission for Latin America just after World War II.[2] Since then, dozens of studies have observed similar trends for most commodities.[3] In 1959, for example, it took 24 tons of sugar to purchase one 60 horse power tractor; by 1982, the same tractor cost 115 tons of sugar.[4]

A debate has raged since the 1970s over the causes of

declining terms of trade or, as it is often called, "unequal exchange."[5] Several argued that prices of products entering world trade reflect wage levels in countries where they were produced. Since most developing country goods were produced for export, there was no need to pay workers enough to buy the products, and hence wages and prices remained low. Others placed emphasis on the dominance of developed country corporations over global marketing; still others on the unequal distribution of modern technology.

United Nations economists also demonstrated that transnational corporations which produced commodities like bananas passed productivity raises to Northern consumers in the form of lower prices rather than to Southern workers through higher wages.[6] For many developing countries, deteriorating terms of trade meant chronic trade and balance of payments deficits, requiring external borrowing. The debt crisis begins.

If the roots of debt lie in the post-industrial revolution international division of labor, then the Bretton Woods institutions gave them further nurture. Out of the ashes of World War II and the memory of international economic chaos between the great wars, three institutions were formed as the cornerstones of the postwar economic order: the General Agreement of Tariffs and Trade (GATT) to guide trade; the International Monetary Fund (IMF) to guide finance; and the World Bank to guide growth and production.

Trade

Remedies to declining terms of trade were not within the mandate of GATT. Rather, the organization was set up to deal exclusively with tariff reductions.

By focusing on reducing tariffs, GATT echoed the notion, long a favorite argument of powerful nations, that free trade benefits all countries. These same powerful nations were loath to point out that it was behind high protective tariffs that German and American industries grew to challenge the nineteenth century manufacturing power of Great Britain. Economic historian E.H. Carr, with words as true today as when he wrote them in 1940, pointed out: *"Lassez-faire*, in international relations as in those between capital and labour, is the paradise of the economically strong. State control, whether in the form of protective legislation or protective tariffs, is the weapon of self-defense invoked by the economically weak."[7]

GATT was most relevant to the needs of industrial countries. As tariffs dropped under the guidance of GATT, and as transnational corporations expanded, trade flourished. The value of world trade jumped from $60 billion in 1950 to close to $2,000 billion in 1980.[8] In the process, most developing countries remained dependent on a relatively narrow range of exports to spur economic growth.

Finance

The widespread postwar perception among industrial nations that free market forces ought to govern trade was paralleled in the monetary field by the desire to create an open, stable monetary system based on freely convertible currencies. There were three key features of the financial system that emerged from Bretton Woods. First, the U.S. dollar would act as the primary currency in world trade, and would be convertible into gold at the rate of $35 an ounce. Second, the value of other currencies was pegged to the dollar. Third, the IMF was established as part of the United Nations system to manage this exchange rate system and to make short-term loans to countries with temporary balance-of-payments problems.[9]

Despite the IMF's precipitous growth from 45 original member nations to 148 today, it remains one of the least democratic of all international institutions. Unlike most United Nations agencies, where the one-nation, one-vote principle governs, the IMF assigns votes roughly according to the economic size of each nation. Hence, all black African nations together possess less power than Great Britain. The United States, with 20 percent of total voting power, exceeds the combined total of Latin America and black Africa. Another factor enhancing United States and other developed country power is that the Soviet Union and several Eastern European nations are not members.[10]

The rigid "conditionality" through which the IMF promotes its version of free market economics in the Third World evolved steadily over the last three and a half decades. The Fund's Articles of Agreement state that it is to provide balance-of-payments support "on terms which safeguard its interest."[11] A 1947 IMF agreement with Chile translated safeguards into "appropriate fiscal and monetary measures,"[12] and conditionality was formally born. In 1955, the IMF established the notion of stepped-up conditionality with a ruling: "The larger the drawing in relation to a member's quota the stronger is the justification required of the member."[13]

Conditionality became more important over the next two decades as the Fund's role in the Third World grew. Of particular significance was the creation of the extended fund facility in 1974 (wherein the IMF disbursed loans over three years instead of one), entailing three years of strict IMF supervision. By the 1970s, the usual components of an IMF program included:

- liberalization of foreign exchange and import controls;
- domestic anti-inflationary measures, including curbs on

government spending; freezes on wage increases, and cutbacks on government credits;
- elimination of controls that hold food and consumer goods prices artificially low; and
- greater opening to foreign investment.

In sum, the IMF served as guardian of an international financial order at whose center stood the U.S. dollar. In its increasingly important policy advisor role toward developing countries, the IMF counseled the same free market, export-oriented ideology that the GATT was set up to preserve.

Production

With GATT and the IMF setting the rules of the system, what remained was an institution to promote dynamism and growth.[14] Initially, the Marshall Plan filled this role, with the United States channelling large sums of capital to Western Europe and Japan to rebuild their war ravaged economies. Paving the road for broader multilateralism, the Marshall Plan helped forge a world economy open to U.S., and later European and Japanese, trade and investment.[15]

The World Bank was set up with the parallel goals of promoting projects and productive systems in line with open markets, with emphasis increasingly on the developing world. It was later joined by regional development banks for Latin America, Africa and Asia. Like the IMF, voting shares in these banks were based primarily on economic power; the United States alone holds 35 percent of voting power in the Inter-American Development Bank.

The World Bank quickly set up affiliates to meet different challenges in the Third World. An International Finance Corporation was created to lend to the private sector; an International Development Association handled the least developed nations. By the time of its Tenth Annual Report, the World Bank boasted of success in its efforts: "to put economic and fiscal policies on a sound footing, and to direct public investment in such a way as to promote, rather than obstruct or displace, the flow of private capital."[16]

Viewing export-oriented growth based in good part on external capital as the most dynamic form of development, neither the World Bank, the IMF, nor GATT saw the need to challenge the division of labor that consigned most of the developing world to a weaker, more volatile and dependent role. In this sense, the debt crisis was built into the system.

At the same time, different institutions played different roles in pushing loans, building projects, setting interest rates, shifting capital illegally overseas, and making the other decisions that shaped the crisis in various forms in each country.

Paramount were four sets of institutions that merit closer scrutiny:
- transnational banks and corporations;
- developing country governments and elites;
- developed country governments; and
- international financial institutions.

The role and responsibility of each, in turn, is examined.

Transnational Corporations

Over half of Third World debt (over two-thirds in the case of Latin America) was lent by private transnational banks. While the motivations were many, the original impetus came from the dynamic expansion of transnational corporations overseas, corporations that needed the easy access to finance which only the large private banks could provide. For all the talk of a "free market" and "free competition," the world economy over the past two decades has increasingly fallen under the control of large transnational corporations that exercise power by virtue of their "oligopolistic" and "conglomerate" strength.

An oligopoly refers to a handful of firms that dominate a given market. International oligopolies have emerged over the past decade in automobiles, microprocessors, seeds, petroleum, cigarettes, and many other markets. Conglomerates, firms whose subsidiaries engage in unrelated economic activities, have also become the order of the day. As different markets expand and contract, conglomerates can shift resources into whatever is most profitable at any given time, often with devastating consequences for the workers and communities that are left behind. The immense economic power of these firms is evidenced in the 10-fold increase in sales of the world's top 200 industrial firms over the past two decades, from around $200 billion in 1960 to over $2 trillion in 1980.[17]

Transnational corporations often reinforced the impact of the debt crisis on the poor by contributing to their marginalization and vulnerability. In certain countries, corporations moved in to take over large areas for agribusiness, resulting in less land for domestic food production and higher land costs. As adjacent land became more expensive, it fell into the hands of the rural elite, and increasing numbers of poor and middle peasants were forced to leave their land. This added another stream to the already overcrowded and disease-ridden urban slums, and more people in both rural and urban areas were pushed toward the brink of survival.

Transnational corporations in autos, textiles, and other products have also created global assembly lines, manufacturing parts of a product in one set of countries, assembling it somewhere else, and putting on the finishing touches in yet another. Firms seeking the cheapest labor and most profitable concessions turned certain underdeveloped countries into "export platforms" for light manufactures, pitting one against another in a battle to grant the greatest incentives to foreign corporations.

Despite transnational corporations potential for great contributions to development via training, technology flows and resource transfers, they seldom passed on the know-how for development to institutions or individuals in the developing world. Instead, they sought to maintain firm control over processing, marketing, and distribution. This left many developing countries locked into producing raw materials (that leave millions of peasants dependent on price fluctuations and markets over which they have no control) or engaged in single stages of manufacturing processes.

Such an export orientation required borrowing for agricultural inputs (e.g. fertilizers, pesticides) and industrial raw materials. In addition, the largest transnational corporations' subsidiaries are also substantial borrowers from transnational banks. In 1983, it was estimated that around $100 billion of developing country external debt represented borrowings by the subsidiaries of transnational corporations.[18]

Transnational Banks

Although banking had become transnational as early as the 1870s, the bulk of bank operations and profits in the ensuing century were related to domestic operations. The surge of transnational corporations overseas in the 1950s and 1960s changed that picture, and the quantity of overseas bank lending began to alarm Western governments.

The Kennedy Administration responded in the early 1960s with measures to control the flow of capital out of the United States.[19] American firms with substantial overseas investments in place when the capital controls were introduced responded simply by shifting their borrowing to banks in other countries. The novel feature of this borrowing was that although it was contracted outside the United States, it was denominated in dollars.

If a European bank lent in dollars, it was outside the jurisdiction of U.S. government regulators; since its loans were denominated in dollars, it was not subject to regulation by European authorities. Because this market was initially developed in Europe, it became known as the Euromarket—even as its practice spread to the Bahamas, the Cayman Islands, Singapore, and elsewhere. The beauty of these off-shore banking centers was that the banks enjoyed the advantage of exemption from the usual reserve requirements that central banks impose on commercial banks. Exemption from reserve requirements can make a large difference to short-term bank profits. The Euromarkets also carried the added attraction of guaranteeing the anonymity and secrecy in which bankers flourish. In this atmosphere, the Euromarket grew from $315 billion in 1973 to $2,055 billion in 1982.[20]

The quadrupling of petroleum prices in 1973 poured tens of billions of dollars into this expanding global banking system, much of it to be lent overseas by U.S. banks. The atmosphere was aptly captured by *Time* magazine in 1983:

> After the sharp rise in OPEC's prices in 1973, the process of recycling billions of petrodollars to developing nations became a bonanza for banks. From Wall Street to the financial centers of Western Europe, bankers awoke to the delights of international lending. Eager to win their spurs, young loan officers fell over one another knocking on the doors of finance ministers from Warsaw to Kinshasa. Recalls David Ashby, chief economist at London's Grindlays Bank: 'Bankers like travel and exotic locations. It was certainly more exciting than Cleveland or Pittsburgh, and it was an easier way to make money than nursing along a $100,000 loan to some scrap-metal smelter.'
>
> Annual bonuses and career prospects were at stake; if one bank did not get the business, another would. 'They had to meet specific profit targets,' recalls a senior British financier, discussing U.S. banks in particular. 'They didn't want to hear about the risks. By the time the country couldn't repay, the people who had made the loan were off and away to some other bank.'[21]

Profits from foreign operations for the seven largest U.S. banks soared from 22 percent of total profits in 1970 to 60 percent in 1982.[22] The immense profitability of developing country operations was reflected in Citicorp earning one fifth of its 1982 profits in Brazil, despite having only 5 percent of its total assets there.[23] In certain cases, banks were even able to translate their enormous economic power in developing countries into political power by imposing conditions on loans in a manner usually restricted to the IMF. In Peru, for example, a consortium of banks conditioned a 1976 $200 million loan on Peru accepting an austerity program that included a devaluation, elimination of price controls and spending cuts.[24]

Enthusiastic, cash-rich bankers operating in unregulated markets represent only one side of a loan. Someone must sign the loan agreement on the borrower side. Enter the developing countries.

Developing Country Governments and Elites

Developing countries had entered the Bretton Woods system as second-class citizens, forced to accept decisions made by the industrial powers. A great number of African and Asian countries were still colonies when the system was set up. And, even after independence, their collective voice was minuscule in the new institutions in relation to their population and resources.

Yet, Third World governments and elites must also be held accountable for the debt and their countries' dire economic straits. Many governments and private firms, often with substantial prodding from transnational banks, initiated ill-advised projects. Some managed well; most did not. Many governments listened more to their technocrats than to representatives of their own peasant cooperatives, unions, and women's groups, as they climbed on the World Bank bandwagon of export-oriented growth—cash crops, minerals and, most recently, light manufacturing in the early 1980s.

Erosion of democratic decision-making has been accelerated with the advance of the global financial crisis. Governments have increasingly had to make decisions on an emergency basis in order to meet the demands of banks, corporations, the IMF, and other governments. This political environment has led, in some cases, to increased repression, and is a pressing reminder of the need to address the overall crisis in a global and humane fashion. It should be noted that certain governments that are among the worst perpetrators of economic mismanagement have been kept in power through the political, military, and financial support of some developed country governments.

Attempts to chronicle exactly what developing countries did with the $895 billion that they borrowed must look beyond governments; the private sector was also a sizable customer. There were four major categories of borrowers in most countries—two government and two private: state-owned corporations (primarily in petroleum, steel, energy, mining), national development banks, private sector corporations, and the local private banking system (which again lent the funds to local firms or transnational subsidiaries).

University of California political scientist Jeff Frieden, after a study of Latin American borrowing, argues that sizable portions of the funds were invested productively.[25] He points out that Mexico's state petroleum monopoly (PEMEX), for example, had borrowed about $15 billion by 1981, making it the largest institutional borrower in the Third World. It used that money to finance about half of its exploration, development and petrochemical projects. In Brazil, a large portion of the borrowed funds went into giant infrastructure projects, such as mining complexes in the Amazon, the Itaipu hydroelectric power plant, and a large nuclear power program.[26]

While in a technical sense, these projects might be called "productive," many had an enormously detrimental impact on indigenous populations and the environment. Countless billions in the largest debtor countries (led by Brazil, Chile, South Korea, the Philippines, Pakistan, Egypt, India, and Israel) were also used to build up military industries or import arms which were invariably turned against their own people. According to Ruth Leger Sivard: "Among 20 countries with the largest foreign debt, arms imports between 1976 and 1980 were equivalent to 20 percent of the increase in debt."[27] Led by Brazil, with over $2 billion in annual arms sales abroad, several developing country debtors are now partially repaying banks by exporting arms.[28]

From dams to arms factories, tangible projects account for less than half the debt total in some countries. Much of the rest of the debt is simply unaccounted for, the victim of capital flight, false invoicing or other techniques to send funds to "more secure" havens out of the country. One of the most extreme cases is the Philippines, with a foreign debt of around $27 billion in 1984. U.S. Ambassador to the Philippines Stephen Bosworth estimates that Filipinos have removed more than $10 billion from their country in recent years; the Philippine Center for Research and Communication estimates capital flight at $30 billion since the 1950s, a figure exceeding the total foreign debt.[29]

Millions of dollars of this total moved through holding companies registered in the secrecy of Hong Kong or Curacao. It then was used to buy up condominiums, homes, businesses, and banks. The offenders were executives of large businesses, government cabinet officials, and even the ruling Marcos family. In the words of a senior Filipino executive: "This country has been ruined by the greed of a few people, and what makes me sad is, we can't say enough is enough. We can't seem to bring ourselves to stop them. We're broke; where's the money? There's no accountability. It's sickening."[30]

The Bank for International Settlements (the central banks' central bank, based in Switzerland) estimates that some $50 billion flowed out of Latin America between 1978 and 1982.[31] The U.S. Federal Reserve Board reports that over one-third of the $252 billion increase in the debt of Argentina, Brazil, Chile, Mexico and Venezuela between 1974 and 1982 went into buying assets overseas or was deposited in foreign bank accounts.[32] Even as the government in Buenos Aires announced that it could not service its foreign debt in the middle of 1982, one of Argentina's richest property developers, the Macri Group, was developing a $1 billion luxury apartment complex in Manhattan. Mexican government statistics suggest that

Mexicans own some $25 billion worth of property in the United States and have about $20 billion deposited in U.S. banks.

Clearly not all Third World governments and elites channelled debt into ill-advised projects and capital flight. Some borrowing did end up in the infrastructure projects so vital to more indigenously-oriented development. Unfortunately, for the majorities in the developing world, such operations were few and far between, and hence a good portion of the blame for the debt debacle lies on the shoulders of developing country elites and governments. Their counterparts in the developed world, however, must share the blame.

Developed Country Governments

Besides supporting dictatorships in debtor nations from Chile to the Philippines, Western governments, led by the United States, have contributed to the debt crisis in three ways. First, U.S. economic policies in the 1960s undermined the role of the dollar in the Bretton Woods system and encouraged the growth of private overseas lending. The age of fixed exchange rates was replaced by an unstable system of floating exchange rates where a "strong dollar" could add substantially to the burden of developing country trade and debt payments transacted in dollars.

Secondly, governmental development assistance declined as private lending markets grew in the 1970s, and governments failed to set regulations on these expanding private markets. Finally, U.S. fiscal and monetary policies since the late 1970s created huge budget deficits and high interest rates, adding billions of dollars of debt service payments to Third World debtors.

Each of these merits further explanation.

Collapse of the Bretton Woods Rules

Central to the Bretton Woods system was the role of the dollar as the currency of international trade and its convertibility into gold. The system operated smoothly for the United States in the 1950s and early 1960s before running into trouble. Despite U.S. trade surpluses throughout the 1960s, the U.S. gold began to stream out of Fort Knox. Several factors were at play: the United States sent large amounts of capital overseas in the form of aid in the 1950s and 1960s (first primarily to Europe and then the Third World); the United States began spending large amounts on the Vietnam War, sums that would total around $150 billion between 1950 and 1975; and there was a substantial increase in foreign investment by U.S. firms, far greater than the inflow of investment into the United States from Europe and Japan.

The resurgence of Europe and Japan provided a challenge to U.S. exports in world markets, and more money began leaving the United States than was coming in. By the end of the 1960s, the deficit on the U.S. balance of payments reached $4.5 billion annually. Since the dollar was pegged to gold, gold began to move from Fort Knox to Europe, and by the end of the decade, U.S. gold reserves were half their 1950 level.[33] In 1970, Nixon lowered interest rates in an attempt to stave off recession, and even more capital flowed out of the United States to earn higher returns overseas.

The rise of transnational banks and the Euromarkets helped speed the capital flight, marking the beginning of a key shift from international financial transactions being guided primarily through the Bretton Woods institutions towards the primacy of unregulated private markets. By 1971, the U.S. balance of payments deficit surpassed $10 billion, and the gold exodus reached unacceptable levels. To stem this resource transfer, Nixon suspended the convertibility of the dollar into gold, and the major currencies were forced to float against one another.

While the demise of the dollar-gold relationship was not mourned by developing countries, it ushered in a period, which continues to this day, of continual instability in financial markets. The value of developing country currencies *vis-a-vis* the dollar became as uncertain as the export prices of their primary commodities. And, as with commodity prices, developing countries exercised no control over the shifting value of their currencies.

Both a "weak dollar," which raises the relative cost of U.S. imports, and a "strong dollar," which reduces demand for U.S. exports, can be destabilizing in the Third World. The point of balance or equilibrium—ever shifting—is difficult to locate, much less sustain. Debt grew fastest in a period of a "weak dollar." As the dollar was to become "stronger and stronger" in 1983 and 1984, it took more and more *pesos, dinars, kwachas* or *rupees* to service dollar-denominated external debt.

Declining Foreign Assistance

As private financial markets grew, official (i.e. from governments) assistance began to decline. In the first two postwar decades, the United States had been a leader in international assistance, first with the Marshall Plan, and then through the Agency for International Development and the Alliance for Progress in Latin America. Other developed countries also set up ambitious aid programs and by the early 1960s, developed countries allocated half of one percent of their gross national product to aid.[34]

With the breakup of the Bretton Woods system and the general slowdown of the world economy in the 1970s, aid levels fell off. Since the 1970s, developed country aid has fluctuated around a third of one percent of gross national product. The United States donates a mere quarter of one percent.[35] Viewed through another prism, official aid dropped dramatically from 54 percent of total capital inflow into developing countries in the 1960s to 32 percent in 1970 to 23 percent in 1982.[36] In the absence of abundant official aid, developing countries turned increasingly to private capital markets.

Was this shift detrimental to development interests in developing countries? Many of the criticisms about export dependence, insensitivity to the poor and the environment can be leveled against both private loans and governmental aid. Private loans, however, have four notable disadvantages from the standpoint of debt-ridden developing countries. First, they tend to have far shorter repayment periods, much of it under one year. At the end of 1981, for example, close to 80 percent of Latin America's debt was private. Much of it was also short-term: 49 percent of Mexico's private bank debt, 61 percent of Venezuela's, and 47 percent of Argentina's were due within a year.[37] Second, most private bank debt is contracted at variable interest rates, and as U.S. interest rates climb, so does developing country debt service.

Third, private bank lending interest rates have always been higher than those on loans from the World Bank and bilateral donors. Finally, and most importantly, private lending goes to what is immediately profitable; it does not go to rural development for the poor or social services of any sort.

Hence the decline of developed country aid exacerbated the debt crisis by pushing developing countries onto more unstable and short-term private markets. Developed country governments can be further faulted for not taking responsibility in regulating the excesses of the Euromarket and other private markets as they grew with abandon after the early 1970s.

Recent Fiscal and Monetary Policy

Despite the relative decline in U.S. economic power in the world as Europe and Japan surged onto world markets in the 1970s, the U.S. economy still has an enormous impact on the global economy. And, U.S. fiscal and monetary policies, set primarily for their domestic impact, can have an inordinately large impact on developing countries. Several shifts in U.S.

fiscal and monetary policies over the past decade have either encouraged borrowing or increased the debt service burden in the Third World.

First, monetary policy between 1975 and 1979 kept interest rates relatively low. Hence, developing countries with high inflation rates faced very low costs of borrowing, a factor which encouraged even greater dollar-denominated borrowing by Third World countries.

Following a period of alarming capital outflow from the United States, the Federal Reserve Board reversed previous policy in the fall of 1979 and began putting a very tight squeeze on the growth of money and credit for the next three years. Relatively quickly, interest rates hit a record level of 15 percent, and capital was attracted back into the United States. This move by the Federal Reserve also contributed to slowing the U.S. economy down and with it, the world economy. The slowdown decreased demand for developing country exports and between 1980 and 1982, prices of primary commodities relative to industrial goods fell some 40 percent.[38] This slammed the brakes on both development projects and debt service payments.

The new Reagan Administration continued the tight monetary policies of Carter, and soon interest rates topped 20 percent.[39] In 1981, Reagan and Congress made a radical shift in fiscal (tax and spending) policies. The 1981 budget granted huge tax cuts to both corporations and higher income people which were scheduled to expand over time. In addition, the Department of Defense was allowed to go on a spending spree for weapons. The combination created extraordinary deficits and government borrowing, a demand for funds that could not be met solely by lenders in the United States. The United States had effectively dropped its traditional role of providing financial resources to the rest of the world, and was now drawing funds from them.

By 1985, an annual military budget of $300 billion was the main ingredient of a federal budget that was running $200 billion annual deficits. According to the House Budget Committee: "Clearly, domestic spending is neither uncontrolled nor has it been a principal source of the deficit since 1981. Rather, these deficits have been driven up by the rapid defense buildup, large tax cuts, and the resulting huge and rising interest payments on the debt."[40] Over the next five years, the Reagan Administration plans to spend over $2 trillion on the Pentagon, with nuclear weapons and intervention forces leading the massive buildup. These programs leave neither Americans nor Third World people more secure, and they drain funds from the process of development everywhere.

As a result of the military spending and the massive deficits, relatively high interest rates were still needed to attract Europeans and Japanese to finance the deficit. Those same high real interest rates have added billions of dollars to the servicing charges that Third World nations pay to U.S. banks.[41] In brief, U.S. weapons manufacturers benefit at the expense of Third World people.

In a world economy where the United States plays such a dominant role, there is a critical need to consider the international repercussions of U.S. fiscal and monetary policy. Throughout the postwar period, U.S. authorities have proved singularly callous toward this corollary of their policy.

The IMF and the Crisis Since 1982

In addition to transnational corporations and banks, governments and elites, yet another set of institutions figures prominently in the history of the debt crisis: the multilateral financial institutions, primarily the IMF. The basic structural biases of these institutions were examined earlier in the chapter. They have assumed new roles in the past few years, however, as the debt crisis escalated to new levels of intensity. In many ways, the history of the debt crisis since 1982 has been a history of the IMF, and therefore it is important to consider them together.

The financial crisis broke loudly in 1982, hitting front pages worldwide. There was a sharp rise in bank and business bankruptcies across the industrial world; in May the U.S. brokerage firm Drysdale went under and the Federal Reserve was forced to pump $3 billion into the U.S. banking system.[42] Worse was to follow. The debt crisis came to a head in August when Mexico effectively defaulted on interest payments on its $80 billion foreign debt, and analysts began to look seriously at the size of the numbers involved.

Between 1980 and 1982, Mexico's foreign loans had swelled by an incredible $47 billion. Of the total developing country debt owed to commercial banks in 1982, almost one-half was due to be repaid in a year or less.[43] For the 21 largest non-oil exporting developing countries, the ratio of debt payments to exports had risen from 30 percent in 1973 to 70 percent in 1982.[44] In 1982, the nine largest U.S. banks had outstanding loans to the Third World equal to twice the value of their capital, and their loans to Mexico alone amounted to half the value of their capital.[45]

These banks were anxious to avoid declaring a formal default in Mexico, as this would have forced them to write off their Mexico loans as losses. Enter the IMF, with the assistance of the U.S. Treasury Department, to put together the first of its "jumbo loans"—this one to the tune of $5 billion. No longer was the IMF a short-term lender in cases of temporary balance-of-payment shortfalls. It had become the conductor of a very large orchestra and the stakes were bigger. Brazil followed soon after, and then Argentina, Venezuela and a series of smaller countries unable to meet interest payments. Loans were rescheduled. Terms became more stringent. Repayment periods were shortened.

And, interest rates were raised. In 1980, interest rates on new loans in developing countries were rarely above the London Inter-Bank Offered Rate (LIBOR) plus 1 percent. By 1982-83, the rates were set at 2 percent or more above LIBOR, with refinancing commissions of 1 percent or more.[46] Given the scale of Third World debt, the burden of even small increases in interest rates was onerous. In 1985, an increase in the interest rate of 1 percent would raise the total developing world debt servicing burden by over $9 billion a year, or $25 million a day.

Backed by the Bank for International Settlements and the U.S. Federal Reserve, the IMF became the new international lender of last resort. In dozens of countries, the IMF would exact new promises of reform, give a small loan of its own, and then pressure reluctant private banks to offer new short- and medium-term loans.

While the IMF proved masterful at holding the financial system together, from even a status quo standpoint, new loans were not being provided on an adequate scale to encourage development. In 1983, developing country borrowings were down 24 percent from the 1982 level. That year, Latin America began exporting net capital to its creditors to the tune of $18.4 billion; in 1983, that figure rose to $30.1 billion; in 1984, $26.7 billion.[47] Debt had become a vacuum cleaner, siphoning resources out of the Third World. For governments interested in development, total repudiation of all debt began to look increasingly attractive. No new loans were going into agriculture or basic services; industries were decaying into worthless shells. Debt born of inappropriate growth models was begetting further underdevelopment.

Desperation gave birth to a new approach in 1984. In August of that year, the IMF and its usual cast of extras went to work on Mexico. This time the "deal of the decade" emerged, a $48 billion stretchout of Mexico's 1985-1990 debt burdens through the end of the century. Similar deals followed for Brazil, Argentina, Venezuela, and the Philippines. The World Bank, which had shifted increasingly from project to sectoral loans with conditionality, began to enter the deals as a guarantor of private bank loans. And, the banks let out a collective and premature sigh of relief.

Even the most optimistic scenarios on debt relief project net capital outflows from Latin America continuing through the early 1990s.[48] Many African countries remain on the brink of default. Starvation, deindustrialization, and illegal capital flight remain the rule, not the exception. The poorer majorities in the bulk of developing countries are further from a genuine solution to the debt crisis than they have ever been before.

External Forces and Debt

Where do shocks external to the financial system, such as oil price increases and drought, which are so central to popular versions of the debt crisis, fit in? There is no doubt that they exacerbated the debt build-up, but they did not create it. Nor will their absence make it go away.

The average price of a barrel of oil jumped from $3.22 in 1973 to $33.80 in 1982.[49] For a sugar exporter, the 6.3 tons of oil that a ton of sugar could buy in 1960 were reduced to 0.7 tons by 1982. The 13 tons of oil that a ton of bananas could buy in 1960 were reduced to 1.6 tons in 1982.[50] Developing countries did borrow more to cover the difference, as the international financial system failed to work out a way to transfer the oil surpluses directly to oil importing developing countries without the intermediation of the private banking system.

Likewise, drought is an important component of the massive suffering plaguing the entire Sahelian region of Africa. But in both cases, inappropriate development strategies based on heavy borrowing left the Third World unequipped to deal with external shocks. The drought hit an African region where little agricultural investment had occurred in the previous half decade, and where every available dollar was repaying bank and government creditors. Whereas hundreds of thousands have died in the past during a general African drought, millions face death this time around.

The roots of the international debt crisis penetrate to the core of the international financial system: the ideology of its founders and their preferred growth models; and the decades-long practices of bankers, elites, and government technocrats. These groups of individuals, like actors in a Greek tragedy, all see how their actions are contributing toward disaster, but none acts to alter its behavior.

The time is long past for cosmetic changes. The entire system is in drastic need of reconstruction.

III

An Alternative Policy

Introduction

There can be no durable solution to the debt crisis that does not address the staggering poverty of the majority in most debtor nations. Without an improvement in their welfare, the world economy as a whole will never be healthy or stable. Nor can the crisis be resolved as long as:

- countries' debt burdens are growing faster than their economies;
- IMF medicine further debilitates the patient, rather than offering assistance to meet specific economic problems and development needs;
- policy responses to the debt crisis adversely affect the living standards of workers, farmers, and others in the developed world; and
- an inordinate amount of power in the international financial system remains in private hands, outside the domain of public concerns.

We propose an alternative framework for solutions (elaborated in this final section) that:

- in the *short-term*, alleviates the debt burden of the least developed nations, and redefines rigid IMF conditionality toward more developmental forms of adjustment for all developing countries;

- in the *medium-term*, offers a global package for debt relief; new criteria for bilateral aid, and outlines regulations for private banks; and
- in the *longer-term*, reverts a more democratic IMF to a more modest role of providing short-term balance of payments support in a reformed international financial system.

In addition, we propose new policies in the realm of fiscal and monetary measures, trade, corporate accountability, and agriculture that address not only the needs of Third World populations, but also those of the majority in the United States.

Short- and longer-term measures are equally important. Short-term solutions address the basic survival requirement of those most seriously affected by the crisis. But short-term survival may prove a minor achievement unless the basis for long-term development is laid at the same time.

Is long-term development possible without a basic restructuring of world financial, monetary, and trade systems? This is an issue on which those who drafted this document have varying viewpoints. We share a consensus on the need for global solutions and for a more equitable sharing of the debt burden. Yet, some question whether greater equity can be achieved through institutional reform alone, through continuing to play by rules set down by what they view as inequitable institutions, such as the IMF.

In the three major sections of this chapter, we examine: the principles which should underlie a more equitable international financial system; a critique of the current offering of solutions; and an outline of an alternative set of proposals.

Underlying Principles

Any reforms in established institutions and rules governing the international financial system, or defining new ones, should be based on certain principles. These are principles that reflect and further some of the more noble values upon which the United States was founded. Six can be enumerated.

Democratic Representation and Decision-making

As in the political sphere, so it is true in the economic: power derives its ultimate legitimacy from the consent of the governed. The international financial system, so long dominated by private institutions, needs to be democratized. Increased public authority and democratic controls are necessary if the present inequitable system is to be replaced with a fairer one.

This principle is a key issue at several levels of the world financial system.

Voting power

Currently, representation and voting in international financial institutions such as the IMF are based on economic power: "one dollar, one vote." Thus, the United States and other industrial countries exercise dominant influence over these institutions' decisions, while the vast majority of poorer countries have no real power at all. In accord with democratic principles, voting power in these institutions should reflect the basic United Nations principle of "one nation, one vote."

Management

Management of these institutions and personnel decisions should reflect a more equitable distribution of national representation to replace the current dominance of Western (particularly American and British) personnel. In addition, the current hierarchical nature of international, as well as national, aid agencies is incompatible with effective, democratic practice and thus with developmental results.

Participation in decision-making

At present, only national governments—and indeed, only Finance and Treasury officials—play a direct decision-making role. Yet virtually none of these officials are elected by those who will have to suffer the consequences of their decisions. The United States and other major industrial powers should not be able to enforce their own definitions of development around the world. Ideally, institutions like the IMF and informal fora like the Paris Club should be reshaped to ensure that non-governmental organizations of debtor countries—such as peasant and worker unions—have input into fashioning their countries' adjustment programs. In a similar vein, the concerns of non-governmental organizations in the industrial countries should be reflected in the positions their governments take.

Until informed citizens demand these changes in large numbers, it will be very difficult to affect decision-making in the multilateral institutions. In the meantime, large amounts of development funding should be shifted to national development foundations, private voluntary organizations and other alternative institutions.

Democratic treatment

Democratic treatment implies greater equity in sharing the burden of adjustment in financial crises. Adjustment should not fall disproportionately on the shoulders of vulnerable social groups, especially the poor, who have had the least role in creating the crisis. In addition, the burdens should be shared more equitably among countries as well as social groups. Bank and IMF concessions offered to the largest debtor countries should not be withheld from smaller debtors, as they have been up to now.

Accountability

Accountability is intertwined with the principle of democracy. International financial institutions, private commercial banks and the individuals that run them must become more accountable to the public in both North and South. Lack of accountability undermines democracy's substance, if not its form. Such accountability requires:

- far greater public knowledge of, and involvement with, these institutions;
- mechanisms whereby U.S. citizens, for example, can make their concerns heard by the U.S. executive directors to these institutions;
- mechanisms for arbitration when weaker governments have grievances against their treatment by these institutions and by the stronger governments that dominate them; and
- regulatory mechanisms to insure more socially responsible operations by banks, which are currently accountable only to their shareholders.

Universality

Given the growing economic interdependence among nations, all countries should be members of major international financial institutions. Universality also requires ending discrimination within the institutions against nations whose social and economic systems and macro-economic goals differ from those of the dominant Western powers.[1]

Guarantee of Fair Reward for Labor

This principle is relevant to all institutions governing the world economic order, whether they govern finance, trade, or development. At the level of *national economies*, the world economic system should guarantee fair and remunerative prices to the developing country producers of raw materials, and institutions should be reformed or built anew to further this principle. At the level of the *individual laborer*, decisions by institutions (banks and the IMF) should not undermine labor rights. Currently, IMF programs often seek to reduce real wages and reinforce government repression of workers seeking better wages or working conditions. Democratic societies could hold public debates to build a social consensus on the definition of fair reward; without real democracy, principles of equity will remain dreams.

Priority to Meeting Basic Human Needs

Development that meets basic human needs should inform solutions. This implies a critical look at existing models—primarily export-led growth—currently promoted by international financial institutions.[2] Export-led growth has carried as a corollary the erosion of basic human needs. The cooperation of Third World governments with local and international private interests in a triple alliance has meant that none of the three is beholden to or likely to serve the needs of the poor. Encouraging developing countries to become self-reliant in food production is a key component to insure that countries can weather balance of payments storms with their people's welfare intact.

Equity in Sharing Losses

Central to this report, and related to the principles of democracy and accountability, is the issue of equity. The costs of the $895 billion of Third World debt will be paid by someone. They must, however, be lifted from the poorer majorities and shared more fairly. This requires an end to disguising the problem, to maintaining the fiction that the bulk of these loans are still "'performing'' in any meaningful way. Creditor as well as debtor countries need to bear some of the costs, along with the world's transnational bank lenders. U.S. taxpayers who have begun to pay for the crisis should not pick up the tab of those banks and corporations whose irresponsibility or short-sightedness helped create the crisis. More responsible and accountable corporate behavior can only be secured through more meaningful public regulation of the banks.

The public has the right and obligation to hold up any proposal against these standards and judge whether it enhances public authority, accountability, equity and development. It is on the foundation of these principles that the range of proposed solutions to the debt crisis are assessed, and that new proposals for resolving the crisis and advancing development are offered.

Evaluation of Current Proposals

This section reviews four major schools of thought which have emerged concerning solutions to the debt crisis:

- solutions framed within the existing international financial system;
- solutions which provide for the expansion of existing financial institutions or the establishment of new ones that help reform the system;

- proposals from developing countries; and
- more long-run solutions which provide for structural reforms in the international financial system.

Solutions Framed Within the Existing Financial System

Major commercial banks and leading industrial country governments (e.g. the United States, United Kingdom, West Germany) largely believe that the quick reaction by governments, central banks, and private banks to crises as they arise in different countries is itself an effective solution. The assumption is that developing countries suffer a short-run liquidity (cash-flow) problem. In the words of economist William Cline: "If this growth rate [3 percent annually for industrialized countries] can be achieved, the debt problems of the developing countries should be manageable and should show considerable improvement . . . The central result of this analysis is that the debt problem can be managed, and that it is essentially a problem of illiquidity, not insolvency."[3]

With further assistance from the IMF and after appropriate adjustment policies, debtors will be able to service their debts and finance expansion. The creditor banks maintain that existing methods and institutions are capable of managing the situation; they express concern that any comprehensive solution which requires a complete restructuring of international debt could spark the very crisis that it is designed to avoid.

Proposals

Their proposals are based on three assumptions: continued lending to developing countries, albeit at a reduced level; a stronger IMF requiring strict conditionality; and a sustained world economic recovery[4].

Private bank confidence in this approach is reinforced by the belief that most of the necessary economic adjustment has already taken place. Banks assume that the IMF will see to it that banks continue to lend enough to tide developing countries over (about $20 billion annually by some estimates).[5] They feel certain that the Third World can adjust to this level of lending because there is still room for increased "efficiency" in the way these domestic economies are managed. Banks point to a series of "inefficient" policies and symptoms of such policies that retard economic growth in developing countries—overvalued exchange rates, high domestic inflation, negative real interest rates, high wages, discrimination against foreign corporations, import-substitution policies, and inefficient state enterprises. Banks argue that by changing these policies and by opening economies more to transnational investors, countries can adjust to lower levels of international lending without a major slowdown of their economies.

Evaluation

Debt moratoria and dramatic breakdowns have so far been avoided. But, from a development standpoint, the situation continues to deteriorate. This first approach offers no new arrangements to provide an increased flow of funds for the future. Inability to service debts by a number of debtor governments is being papered over by rescheduling deals that substitute future promises to pay for what are in reality defaults on payments.

These piecemeal arrangements reflect none of the six principles for an international financial system that advances development and the needs of the poorer majorities. If solutions framed within the existing international financial system continue to be the major response of governments and banks to the crisis, development prospects will continue to erode. There will be no public checks on banks that will be bailed out on the backs of the poor. Social unrest will increasingly be the response from the Third World.

Solutions that Extend the Role of Financial Institutions

Some investment bankers, liberal economists, and political leaders are convinced that the debt crisis is more than a temporary liquidity shortage and believe that existing methods may not be able to resolve it. Therefore, in addition to the recommendations listed above, they have proposed a wide range of solutions which provide for the expansion of existing financial institutions or the establishment of new ones.[6] The adherents of this approach disagree with one another mainly on the question of who should be forced to pay for cleaning up the debt debacle.

Proposals

Proposals to create or extend financial institutions to assume some of the risk on international loans are predicated on two assumptions: that a major portion of these loans will never be repaid, and that the world economy will not recover until the debt burden is reduced.

One set of these proposals is laid out comprehensively in the Brandt Commission report, the product of an independent commission on international development issued under the direction of former West German Prime Minister Willy Brandt.[7] The report focused on supplementary financing for the Third World through an increase in IMF resources and more use of co-financing with private lenders.

The Commission argued that the world needs a substantial increase in resource transfer from the developed to the developing world in order to alleviate poverty, to expand food production and domestic processing of commodities, and to generate new development projects. It proposed passage of international agreements to stabilize the prices and earnings of commodity exports.

Another prominent reform proposal is that of Felix Rohatyn, an investment banker who is best known as the mastermind who resolved the 1970s New York City financial crisis.[8] Rohatyn wants to convert developing country short-term debt into longer-term obligations by means of a new public international creditor agency that would buy the existing debts from the commercial banks. This new creditor could be an expanded IMF or World Bank or a new agency, and would exchange present short- to medium-term debt obligations for its own long-term, low-interest bonds. The private banks would suffer a loss of current income, but Rohatyn believes that the subsequent upgrading of the credit would give bank regulators a basis for allowing the banks to schedule limited write-offs of losses over a long period of time.

Variations on the Rohatyn scheme have been put forward by academics (such as Princeton economist Peter Kenen), politicians (such as New Jersey Senator Bill Bradley), and former government officials (Henry Kissinger).[9] All include provisions for the government to inject new funds, a new process for debt rescheduling, and some write-off of principal and profits by commercial banks.

Evaluation

The merit of these proposals is that they take the problem of debt out of the case-by-case, crisis management mode and put it into an institutional channel where the rules are clear. The banks accept some short-term losses, but are let off the hook. Confidence is restored in the banking system by making profit write-offs orderly.[10] A disadvantage is that taxpayer funds would have to be used to bail out banks for mistakes largely of the banks' own making, without increasing the public authority over banks that might prevent a repeat of the past mistakes.

Other proposals to increase IMF resources and lending substantially have been criticized as mechanisms to allow private banks to shift their least prudent loans to the IMF. Again, governments (through their appropriations to banks), and taxpayers in the developed countries would bear the costs.

None of these approaches address the debt problem in all its complexities and in its relationship to the development process. Allocation of losses and costs among bank stockholders and creditor country taxpayers is usually left ambiguous. None of the schemes address the question of how to get new funds into developing countries; it is hard to imagine banks continuing to lend to developing countries after they have incurred major short-term losses. None address the basic issue of how to raise the quality of development and democracy in both North and South.

In terms of the six principles we have established for an equitable reform of the system, some of the proposals state that the policies of the new government agency should be more geared to growth and development in the Third World, and that the burden for paying some of the debt should be transferred from developing to developed countries. In no other respects, however, do these proposals advance public authority, accountability, or equity.

Proposals from the South: Regional Cooperation

In recent years, a flurry of proposals that address the debt crisis have been advanced in the Third World, from both governments and opposition forces. Following three years of painful austerity and negative growth, many governments in Africa[11] and Latin America have spoken out against the programs of the IMF and foreign commercial banks. In a series of regional meetings, from Arusha to Quito to Cartegena, African and Latin American leaders have discussed collective solutions to deal with their economic crises.

The various cooperation schemes call for sharing the burden of responsibility for the debt crisis and recognizing that both internal and external factors were at its root. According to the schemes' proponents:

- Third World countries have already made extraordinary adjustments in their economies in order to meet international obligations;
- it is now the turn of the banks, creditor countries, and the IMF to do the same;
- economic growth is to take priority over servicing of foreign debt; and
- the social costs of future adjustment programs should be minimized.

Most of these proposals have been put forward in Latin America. Other than Fidel Castro, no Latin American head of state has officially proposed setting up a debtors' cartel or called for a unilateral repudiation of the debt (as of July 1985). But, a number of proposals have been put forward suggesting alternative actions.

Prominent among the proposals is to pay debt service only up to a fixed percentage of export earnings.[12] Terms of repayment is another thorny issue often addressed. A 1984 meeting of finance and economy ministers from eleven Latin American debtors in Cartagena, Columbia[13] called for:

- international policies that would reduce interest rates;
- temporary mechanisms to reduce the impact of high interest rates, including a new IMF facility for this purpose;
- improved terms of lending through longer maturities and grace periods, and multi-year reschedulings;
- a shift in IMF programs toward greater priority on production and employment; and
- elimination of trade barriers in industrial countries, along with efforts to stabilize commodity prices.

Whether Third World calls for a constructive dialogue to discuss such proposals are heeded or fall on deaf ears will depend upon the banks and legislatures of the West and the state of Western economies. Most bankers and U.S. government officials argue against regional cooperation efforts. "The best way to resolve country debt negotiations is on a bilateral basis," asserts Citibank Vice President George Clark.[14] Bankers oppose blanket concessions to all countries and proceed on a divide and rule basis. They argue that only those countries such as Mexico, that comply with the austerity measures prescribed by the IMF, should receive lower interest rates and longer terms on their debt reschedulings. A spokesperson for the U.S. Treasury Department, Brian Benson, stated the "the differences among the debtor countries are so great in financial and economic terms that we are doubtful that any regional or global plan will go very far."[15]

Proposals from the South are likely to be taken seriously by Northern bankers and government officials only if several countries announce a moratoria on debt payments or if there is a substantial recession in the North which further exacerbates the global economic crisis.

Long-term Solutions for Structural Reform

A third school of thought on the debt crisis addresses itself to more thorough long-term solutions. It includes the proposals for a New International Economic Order (NIEO) debated in the United Nations since 1974, and proposals put forward by those who feel developing countries should distance themselves further from the world market.

Most industrial countries have been reluctant to implement policies designed to share the world's resources more equitably with the South. Developing country governments responded to this recalcitrance in May 1974 with a Declaration and Action Programme on the Establishment of a New International Economic Order before the United Nations General Assembly. The Declaration called for fundamental changes in the operation of the international economy, including major changes in the role and practices of private international banks and the IMF. More specific calls for structural reform of the system have come from a conference in Arusha, Tanzania in 1980,[16] developing country forums such as the Group of 77, the United Nations Conference on Trade and Development, the World Council of Churches,[17] and grassroots organizations.

Proposals

A useful reference point in discussing NIEO proposals is the position taken by the "Group of 24," the 24 developing countries that meet to hammer out a joint Third World position in the IMF. In its 1983 "Outline Program of Action on International Monetary Reform,"[18] the Group of 24 called for:

- the expansion of developing country quotas in the IMF from 30 to 50 percent of the total voting power;
- an expansion of balance of payments support on low conditionality terms for developing countries;
- a medium-term IMF facility providing finance on concessional terms; and
- an increased allocation of Special Drawing Rights (SDRs) to developing countries.

Other proposals for radical change have started from the premise that fewer linkages with the world economy would be beneficial for developing countries in preventing future debt crises and in advancing development. Critics of the current international financial system such as Cheryl Payer and Theresa Hayter (from a political economy perspective), and the German Green party (from an ecological perspective) have put forward analyses along these lines.[19]

Another set of proposals have focused on the fact that the supply of "hard currencies"—those currencies used as international reserves and for trade—is determined by the economic policies of a few industrial nations, primarily the United States. Hence, exchange rate stability and the provision of sufficient liquidity to facilitate world economic development is out of the control of developing countries. This observation has led to proposals that SDRs should replace the U.S. dollar and other Western currencies as the main form of "hard currency." The supply of SDRs would be decided democratically by a new World Central Bank.[20]

Such a World Central Bank would need to be universal in membership, including socialist countries. Further, it would need to be democratic in structure, and would have to be capable of accommodating itself to countries with widely divergent social and economic systems.

Evaluation

There are generally two types of reform advocated in the NIEO approach. One seeks through various means to provide the IMF with substantially more resources to lend to developing countries. The other is more radical, granting developing countries greater scope in choosing among development models. This second type implies acceptance of non-capitalist development strategies, and calls for a democratically determined supply of "world money," greater developing country voting rights in the IMF, and greater transfers from developed to developing countries.

The first type of reform without the second would not insure development in the long run. Massive new lending without changing the conditions for loans would further the pattern of dependence by opening economies further and discouraging more self-reliant industrialization. Developing countries would continue to rely on foreign capital for productive investment to provide employment, raise output, and increase exports, and would continue to suffer the effects of capital outflows. In addition, most of the increased aid would continue to flow into servicing existing debts[21].

While the broader Group of 24 proposals would tend to make the IMF more democratic and responsive to development needs, they do not satisfy the principles of accountability, universality, equity in sharing losses, and labor rights. The more fundamental NIEO reforms come a step closer to both the principles and the United Nations' vision of an economic order:

> based on equity, sovereign equality, interdependence, common interest and cooperation among all States, irrespective of their economic and social systems, which shall correct inequalities and redress existing injustices, make it possible to eliminate the widening gap between the developed and the developing countries and ensure steadily accelerating economic and social development and peace for present and future generations.[22]

Finally, proposals for a World Central Bank carry the advantage of addressing basic structural weaknesses in the international financial system. Such a bank could be consistent with the principles of democratic representation, accountability and universality, and could induce more responsiveness to Third World development concerns. It remains unclear, however, how the bank would be financed.

Despite the weaknesses, several proposals among this final set begin to address the roots of debt and underdevelopment.

A New Alternative

If the goal is not only debt relief but also participatory development that benefits the poorer majority, a more comprehensive
approach to solutions is needed. As Americans, there are many
avenues through which debt and development can be addressed. As shareholders and consumers, we can influence the
activities of private banks and corporations and reshape the
education system and media to encourage greater citizen participation.

As voters and citizens, we can influence the activity of
Congress. Congress, in turn, has regulatory authority over the
banks, and is a major actor in fiscal, monetary, trade, and other
policy. Through the granting of foreign aid, the Congress also
has a heavy influence on development in the Third World.
Finally, through Congressional replenishments and U.S. executive directors to the international financial institutions, we
have some influence over the activities of the IMF, World Bank
and regional development banks for Africa, Asia, and Latin
America.

These proposals are offered as guidelines for an alternative
approach. We have refrained from greater specificity since once
there is a larger political consensus to adopt any of the general
policies, the specific means will be hammered out.

Short-term Measures

For short-term alleviation of the suffering of the most vulnerable groups in the developing world, it is useful to distinguish
three groups of developing countries with different needs and
requiring different treatment.

The Most Seriously Affected Countries

The United Nations has identified 36 countries which, by its
criteria, are the "least developed" in the world. Most are
currently suffering food crises affecting large portions of their
populations, and are badly in need of immediate debt relief.
These 36 countries collectively owe only $26.2 billion (1982),
only 2.9 percent of Third World debt, and most of it is owed to
government sources.[23] In order to save tens of thousands of
lives, Western governments should follow the lead of those
Scandinavian governments that have transformed outstanding
debt to some of these countries into grants. New credit should
be made on easier terms to ease the immediate suffering.
Western banks could carry out a similar debt forgiveness with
only a minor impact on earnings.[24]

Safeguards have been proposed to insure that debt cancellation is not followed by the same borrowing practices that
created the crisis at the expense of development. The West

German Green Party, for example, suggests that interest and principal write-offs be paid (in local currencies) by debtor countries into a national development fund managed by non-governmental organizations (e.g. farmers associations, unions, consumer groups, women's groups). The fund would finance self-reliant development projects which aim to satisfy basic needs.

Flagrant Development and Human Rights Violators

A second group includes those few countries where government disregard for the development conditions of the country and the basic needs of the majority is so blatant that the world community advocates a total halt to all new loans to their governments. At present, broad consensus exists on South Africa, and there is a growing consensus on Chile, Zaire, the Philippines, and Guatemala, and elsewhere. Emphasis should be placed on channeling assistance to non-governmental groups in these countries.

The Remaining Debtors

A third group includes the majority of developing countries, which fall between the first two categories. The U.S. executive director to the IMF (and to the World Bank with respect to non-project lending) should support a new developmental version of conditionality for these nations that would guide the use of resources to assure that they do not go down the drain like so much of the money lent during the 1970s. In particular, before voting in favor of a loan, the U.S. executive director should be satisfied that:

- the country has provided a development plan tailored to its specific resource base, infrastructure, development goals, and problems. The plan must have economic targets that are feasible, unlike the majority of IMF plans for debtor countries in 1984, which were violated soon after going into effect.

- the U.S. executive director to the Fund, in accordance with U.S. law (PL96-369 of 1980),[25] should only vote for those loans where the plan submitted adequately provides for: creating safe, healthy, and environmentally sound jobs; narrowing the gap in wealth and income between rich and poor; and advancing health, housing, education, and other basic human needs.

- two other considerations, not designated by the 1980 law, should be added. First, the economic plan should specify measures to redress the severe impact of the debt on vulnerable groups, particularly women and children. Second, the plan should demonstrate that natural resources (forest, wetlands, agricultural lands) are conserved and managed for sustainable development.

- the plan must demonstrate the ability of the country to repay the loan and to continue servicing its debt, as long as service payments do not exceed 20 percent of the country's export earnings. Even these payments should be seen as short-term; in the medium-term, a more thorough debt cancellation and loss sharing plan is proposed.

All letters of intent to the IMF should also spell out the projected impact of economic adjustment policies on jobs, wealth distribution, and basic needs. The secrecy surrounding these programs should also be eliminated. Adjustment programs and IMF loans are supposed to be in the interest of developing country recipients, and taxpayers from all over the world pay for the loans. The IMF should therefore make public the contents of adjustment programs.

Medium-term Measures

In the medium-term, the United States should adopt policies which discourage the kind of lending that fueled the debt crisis and should address ways to decrease the overall level of debt. It can do this primarily through bilateral lending policies and banking legislation. First, however, it needs to address the central issue of debt relief and loss sharing.

Debt Relief and Loss Sharing

None of the above measures significantly reduces the $895 billion Third World debt looming over the entire system. Politically, this larger question is unlikely to be seriously addressed in an international forum before the next major recession in the United States and world economy. When that occurs, we should be ready to launch proposals for bankers, government officials, and representatives of non-governmental organizations—under the auspices of the United Nations—to bring to the table. They should include:

- proposals to convert parts of official debt (i.e. debt to government institutions) and parts of the private debt into grants;[26]
- proposals for a multi-year moratorium on debt servicing of both public and private debt and a significant extension of periods for consolidating and repaying the remaining overdue debt service over the longer-term; and
- proposals to repay some of the debt "in kind." One such form of repayment that might be explored is the preparation of packages of "services" such as conservation of species (genetic) diversity in biological reserves and national parks.

Just as the current patchwork approach to solutions involves losses borne largely by poor and working peoples, so too will these proposals involve large losses as portions of the debt are written off. Negotiations among banks, developed country governments and developing country governments will be necessary to work out how losses will be shared among the three groupings. Public pressure will be essential to insure that the taxpayers' contribution to the loss sharing is compensated with an increase in public authority over the nation's banking system.

Bilateral Aid

As outlined in the earlier chapters, U.S. aid policies have tended to exacerbate the debt crisis. U.S. loans have generally been channelled into export-oriented projects compatible with the overall growth philosophy of the IMF and World Bank. This export-led model has depended upon heavy borrowing from abroad.

An overhaul of U.S. aid policies can be reshaped along the following guidelines that encourage participatory development:[27]

Aid should be channelled to institutions that encourage greater self-reliance in developing countries and among the poorer majorities. U.S. assistance should support, not discourage, developing country efforts to diversify economic activities away from reliance on trade toward those that provide employment opportunities in areas that benefit the local population. Such activities might include: public works projects that renew ecosystems or develop needed infrastructure with minimal reliance on imports, and projects that enhance food production for local consumption. These include measures to insure more equitable land distribution; a greater focus on the needs of small, subsistence farmers (particularly women) and agricultural laborers; and a shift from export-oriented and large agribusiness production to staple food production.

Democratically managed rural credit organizations could be encouraged that support expanded agricultural processing, packaging, storage, marketing and transportation. Small-scale village industries that employ local materials, technology, and skills could also be given priority, particularly those which generate employment for women.

Aid policies should support better representation and involvement of the poor in economic decisions and development activities affecting their lives. The poor need to participate in defining the problem as well as in project design, implementation and evaluation. Many Third World governments and economic institutions do not represent poor and working people; in these countries, it is essential that the United States develop much greater sensitivity to local conditions so that it can channel its aid to those organizations which do. This is one avenue whereby poor people can gain a louder voice in policies which affect them. U.S. aid policies can encourage more democratic decision-making structures by funding community development projects and cooperatives run by workers and peasants themselves.

Reduce military and security-related assistance and raise development assistance. Security assistance is often a direct response to the need by certain Third World governments to repress unrest among the population, unrest often fueled by austerity borne of the debt crisis. The needs of the people would obviously be better met if much of the amount spent on military aid was instead spent on long-term economic development. What does it mean for U.S. economic relations with the rest of the world that "security assistance" accounts for 69 percent of foreign aid authorizations in the 1986 budget, compared to 55 percent in 1981? In most cases the answer is simple: more debt and more repression.

End use of the U.S. aid for political and domestic economic aims. Often, aid is used to further U.S. financial and direct investment in the developing world or is tied to the purchase of U.S. goods and services. The United States has also politicized multilateral aid agencies such as the World Bank by diverting resources from countries whose political or economic systems do not meet U.S. approval. Instead, development and basic human needs criteria should form the basis for U.S. policy decisions within multilateral financial institutions.

Oppose linking aid to a country's acceptance of IMF conditions. Such linkage renders U.S. bilateral aid subject to the inappropriate, harmful conditions pushed by the IMF.[28]

Policy toward Banks

Banks have added to the crisis in recent years by charging high interest rates on new loans that have essentially been used to service old loans. Banks could be pressed to write off, or convert into grants, interest payment arrears accumulated as a result of recent interest rates increases. Congressman Charles Schumer and economist Alfred Watkins have calculated that 70-80 percent of the new loans to many of the largest debtors since 1979 have been used to pay interest on old loans, and hence have had nothing to do with development.[29] To reverse this practice, they have proposed that: "banks should be forbidden to report profits on any foreign loans on which the banks are lending borrowers the money to pay interest. This will not only reduce the rewards for loaning money to pay back loans; it will also give banks an incentive to lower their interest rates to levels that debtor nations can pay without taking out new loans."[30]

Other legislative measures toward banks that would help ease repayment burdens include requirements on banks to cap loan renegotiation fees and interest rates charged to the poorest countries, as originally proposed by Schumer in 1983.

Longer-term Measures

In the longer term, once the immediate crisis is over, we would urge that a reformed and democratized IMF be reduced to a far more modest task of coordinating the foreign exchange policies of its members and of responding to their truly short-term liquidity needs. Or, as clearly spelled out in the Fund's Articles of Agreement, "to make financial resources available to members, on a temporary basis and with adequate safeguards, to permit them to correct payments imbalances without resorting to measures destructive of national and international prosperity." Indeed, the prosperity clause is certainly violated in current IMF "austerity" packages.

Other U.S. Policies

This overall alternative should be pursued in conjunction with proposals to change certain related facets of U.S. macro-economic policy, particularly in the fields of: fiscal and monetary policy, trade, transnational corporations, and agriculture.

Fiscal and Monetary Policy

The United States could reduce the debt servicing burden on Third World countries by putting its own house in better order. The enormous U.S. budget deficits could be reduced by cutting defense spending and by restoring taxes on corporations and persons with higher incomes.

By reducing the deficit and therefore government borrowing,[31] the United States could more easily reduce interest rates. That would quickly relieve some of the Third World's debt servicing burden since most of the debt has variable interest rates (pegged to the U.S. prime rate) or is short-term.

The United States should also agree to demands from abroad to work on a new system of more stable exchange rates. Almost every trading partner, both developed and developing, believes that the current system must be changed to prevent the wild gyrations of exchange rates that have occurred in recent years.

Trade

Behind its "free trade" rhetoric, the Reagan Administration has no coherent trade policy. Rather, its monetarist stringency budget deficit/high interest rate policies have contributed to a strong U.S. dollar. Tax and tariff policies have encouraged transnationals to move production offshore for reimport to the

United States. These policies, in turn, have stimulated increases in U.S. imports and a $123 billion trade deficit in 1984.

A more humane and developmental policy is a socially "managed" trade system which is integrated with a national industrial policy, instead of the current version managed by the Fortune 500 largest corporations. Such an alternative needs to be based on a vision of what the U.S. economy will look like 10 years from now. What parts of our auto, steel, textile, electronics, and aerospace industries will we preserve? Certain industries are moving to the Third World. Should they? If so, we need a transition policy to retrain U.S. workers laid off from these jobs and a reduction in certain trade barriers so that Third World countries in these selected sectors have access to our markets.

It would also seem wise to curb the untrammeled export of jobs by transnationals by removing tax deductions for exports, tax credits for taxes paid to foreign governments, deferrals of profits for tax purposes, and tariff exemptions on goods that transnationals process abroad. Certain of these tax and tariff breaks have, in effect, rewarded Third World governments for exploiting their labor by offering them duty-free entry to U.S. markets. With backing from human rights and labor groups, Congress has amended trade legislation (the Generalized System of Preferences) to deny duty-free access to our markets to countries that violate internationally recognized fair labor standards.[32] A major effort is now needed to insure implementation of this legislation.

Our trade policy toward the Third World is equally destabilizing. The United States has been the leading proponent in the World Bank and IMF of pushing large numbers of developing countries into heavy reliance on exports for growth. The effect has been an increase in human misery since world trade has stagnated in the very period in which some of the poorest countries have been increasing their dependence on exports. At the same time, the United States has placed high barriers against many imports from developing countries. Developing countries might have fared better had they not followed the "experts" advice: Asian nations which emphasized growth in the domestic market along with export growth (India, South Korea) fared better in the early 1980s than those which concentrated solely on exports (Singapore), according to a recent International Labor Organization study[33].

Transnational Corporations

The freedom of transnational corporations to shift capital and jobs at will is often detrimental to U.S. workers and communities and also to the Third World. A well thought out series of regulations are needed to insure accountability of transnationals to workers, communities, and the national government. This could be augmented by institutes and schools to train workers and organizers in worker buyouts, worker ownership, and worker management.

At the very least, legislation requiring corporations to give advance notice to workers on plant closures or decisions to introduce new technologies is essential. A foreign investment review board that reviews applications for large foreign investments in the United States as well as large investments overseas by U.S. corporations would also be helpful.

There is also a need for strong regulations on exports of dangerous drugs and hazardous materials by U.S. corporations. These should be supplemented with regulations which prevent future Bhopals by requiring U.S. corporations to respect U.S. health, safety, and environmental regulations in setting up plants overseas.

Agriculture

Solutions to the "farm crisis" of rural America involve many of the same issues of fiscal, monetary, and trade policy that are central to Third World debt.[34] At the heart of a more just policy on farm debt and the farm crisis should be a sound agriculture policy that would reverse the growing control by non-producers over producers and guarantee renewal of the family farm system;[35] an equitable policy of world food security; a system of resource conservation; and a sound domestic food assistance policy. Such policies should strive for a sustainable, resilient, and economically viable food production and distribution system; enhance diversified ownership of farmland; and guarantee some reasonable stability of income for family farms.

As with Third World debt, certain policy reforms are urgent and others require more serious longer-term planning. In the short term, a system of emergency credit for the most seriously debt-ridden farmers is essential, coupled with a debt restucturing plan for the remainder of family farmers.

In the medium- and longer-term, U.S. tax policy toward family farms should be reexamined to reduce the tax burden. Finally, until the same high U.S. interest rates that have added billions of dollars to Third World and U.S. farm debt are reduced, there needs to be a policy of interest rate relief for farmers.

None of these measures will be accepted without substantial public education and political struggle. Such a struggle can only occur if there are local, regional and national debates on these issues by an informed citizenry. The debate over the debt crisis has far too long been confined to the ranks of bankers, government officials, and a small coterie of economists. Representatives from religious and civil rights organizations, unions, hunger and development groups, the women's movement, environmental agencies, community groups, and others must enter into the fray. Silence from their ranks will only perpetuate debt, poverty, and underdevelopment. Education, debate, and political action are the ingredients of a more humane and democratic alternative.

NOTES

Chapter I

1. Worldwide annual arms expenditures for 1984 are estimated to be $900-970 billion. Annual figures can be found in the yearbooks of the Stockholm International Peace Research Institute (SIPRI), and Ruth Leger Sivard's *World Military and Social Expenditures*.

2. Between mid-1982 and mid-1984, the IMF disbursed $22 billion in adjustment programs in 66 countries. See Azizali Mohammed, "Recent Fund Role in External Debt Management," papers submitted to the United Nations Development Program Vienna Roundtable, September 10-13, 1984; and Azizali Mohammed, "The Case-by-Case Approach to Debt Problems," *Finance and Development* (March 1985), p.29.

3. The combined debt of the largest seven debtors amounted to $385 billion in 1984, around 43 percent of the Third World total. Figures from the Institute of International Finance, quoted in *Wall Street Journal*, May 22, 1985.

4. Figures from background papers prepared for a series of conferences on Central American debt organized by the Latin American Center for Monetary Studies and the Bank of Guatemala in Guatemala City, March 4-6, 1985. Cited in *InterPress Services* wire service, March 28, 1985.

5. Figures from Richard Feinberg, vice president of the Overseas Development Council, in *New York Times*, September 19, 1984.

6. The volume of world exports grew 1.5 percent in 1980; 0 percent in 1981; −2 percent in 1982; and 2 percent in 1983. General Agreement on Tariffs and Trade, *International Trade, 1983/1984* (Geneva: GATT, 1984).

7. See Robin Stainer, "Taking their lumps," *South*, April 1984, p.72; and Jose Galang, "The bitter harvest," *Far Eastern Economic Review*, April 18, 1985, pp.60-63.

8. After credit for purchases of farm inputs, tractors, and other crop services was severely restricted, maize output during the 1978-79 harvest was 44 percent below that of the previous harvest. From Bill Rau, "Conditions for Disaster: The IMF and Zambia," unpublished paper prepared for Interfaith Action for Economic Justice, 1983. For Zambia's ongoing agricultural development disaster, see Guy Gran, "From the Official Future to

a Participatory Future: Rethinking Development Policy and Practice in Rural Zambia," *Africa Today*, Vol 30, No. 4, 1983, pp.5-22. For an excellent introduction to the impact of IMF and World Bank policy on hunger, see Kevin Danaher, "Banking on Hunger, the International Crisis," *Food First News*, Institute for Food and Development Policy, Summer 1984.

9. Calculations from the respected Philippine think tank, the Center for Research and Communication, quoted in *Wall Street Journal*, August 7, 1984.

10. This figure is from a 1985 "State of the World's Women" report written in Kenya, quoted in *Washington Post*, July 6, 1985. See also Christine Obbo, *African Women* (London: Zed Press, 1980), and Edna Bay, ed., *Women and Work in Africa* (Boulder, Colorado: Westview Press, 1982).

11. In 1983, Brazil experienced an annual inflation rate of 200 percent. The government, in compliance with IMF-mandated policies, passed a law making it illegal for employers and unions to negotiate wage increases matching or exceeding the rate of inflation.

12. For details of labor violations in Free Trade Zones, see the Special Order of the U.S. Congress on labor rights in *Congressional Record-House*, August 9, 1984, pp.H8875-H8899.

13. *International Labor Reports* (U.K.), September-October, 1984.

14. Frances Moore Lappe and Joseph Collins, *Food First: Beyond the Myth of Scarcity* (Boston: Houghton Mifflin, 1977), Chapter 7; and the work of the Pesticide Action Network (PAN) of the Malaysia-based International Organization of Consumer Unions.

15. Quoted in *Washington Post*, June 18, 1985.

16. Ernest H. Preeg, ed., *Hard Bargaining Ahead: U.S. Trade Policy and Developing Countries* (New Brunswick, N.J.: Transaction Books, 1985).

17. *New York Times*, series of articles on the farm crisis, February 1-3, 1985; and Jesse Jackson, "Feed the Hungry and Save the Family Farm," speech for Operation PUSH Saturday Forum, January 26, 1985, p.2.

18. *Ibid.*

19. U.S. Department of Agriculture, *The Current Financial Conditions of Farms and Farm Lenders*, Agricultural Information Bulletin No. 490, March 1985.

20. "American Farmers Down the Tubes?" *U.S. News and World Report*, February 4, 1985.

21. "Latin Debt Crunch Hurting U.S. Firms," *Wall Street Journal*, May 8, 1984.

Chapter 2

1. International Monetary Fund and World Bank, *The Problem of Stabilization of Prices of Primary Products* (Washington, D.C., 1969), p.156. For the World Bank's more recent analysis, see World Bank, *Price Prospects for Major Primary Commodities*, 5 volumes (Washington D.C., Report No. 814/84, September 1984).

2. United Nations Economic Commission for Latin America, *The Economic Development of Latin America and Its Principal Problems*, by Raul Prebisch (E/CN.12/89/Rev.1), 1950.

3. The International Center for Development, for example, published a report at the beginning of 1967 which pointed out: "In 1954, a jeep could be purchased with the value of fourteen bags of coffee; by 1962 it required thirty-nine." Quoted in Pierre Jalee, *The Third World in World Economy* (New York: Monthly Review Press, 1969), p.72. See also the publications of the United Nations Conference on Trade and Development (UNCTAD), based in Geneva, Switzerland.

4. Fidel Castro, *The World Economic and Social Crisis*, Report to the Seventh Summit Conference of Non-Aligned Countries (Havana: Publishing Office of the Council of State, 1983), p.62.

5. The debate over "unequal exchange" was carried out most extensively by the French economists Denis, Emmanuel, Bettelheim and Palloix. For a summary of their arguments, see Michael Barratt-Brown, *The Economics of Imperialism* (Middlesex, England: Penguin Books, 1974), Chapter 10. The debate continues and has recently been enriched by American sociologist Stephen Bunker in *Underdeveloping the Amazon: Extraction, Unequal Exchange and the Failure of the Modern State* (University of Illinois, 1985). Bunker argues that assessing labor and capital is insufficient; total energy flows of all sorts must be considered as well.

6. United Nations Conference on Trade and Development, *The Marketing and Distribution System for Bananas* (TD/B/C.1/162), Geneva, 1973.

7. Edward H. Carr, *The Twenty Years Crisis* (London: MacMillan and Co.: 1940), p.77.

8. Compiled by authors from data supplied by the UNCTAD Secretariat, 1983.

9. This discussion draws on T. Evans, "Money Makes the World Go Round," *Capital and Class*, No. 24, Winter 1985.

10. Certain socialist countries have joined the IMF, including: Romania, Vietnam, China, Cambodia, Laos, Yugoslavia, Hungary, and Mozambique.

11. IMF, *Articles of Agreement*, article 5, section 4. See J. Keith Horsefield, ed., *The International Monetary Fund, 1945-1965: Twenty Years of International Monetary Cooperation*, 3 vols. (Washington, D.C.: IMF, 1969).

12. *Ibid.*, Vol. 1, p.192. For details of the IMF's evolution toward

stricter conditionality, see Robin Broad, *Behind Philippine Policy Making: The Role of the World Bank and International Monetary Fund* (Princeton University doctoral dissertation, 1983).

13. Quoted in Horsefield, *op. cit.*, Vol. 2, p.404.

14. For an overall critique of the politics, economics and mythology of growth, see Richard Grossman, "Growth as Metaphor, Growth as Politics," *The Wrenching Debate Gazette*, Nos. 2 & 3, July 1985.

15. Fred Block, *The Origins of International Economic Disorder* (Berkeley, CA: University of California Press, 1977).

16. World Bank, *Tenth Annual Report, 1954-1955* (Washington, D.C., 1955), p.35.

17. Sales of these top 200 jumped from 17 percent of the non-socialist world's gross national product in 1960 to 29 percent in 1980. See John Cavanagh and Frederick Clairmonte, *The Transnational Economy: Transnational Corporations and Global Markets* (Washington, D.C.: Institute for Policy Studies, 1983), p.11.

18. Robert Cohen, "Bank Financing of the Subsidiaries of Transnational Corporations in Latin America," unpublished manuscript, 1984.

19. For details, see Brian Tew, *The Evolution of the International Monetary System, 1945-81* (London: Hutchinson, 1982), p.105.

20. Morgan Guaranty Trust, *World Financial Markets*, July 1983, p.15.

21. Jay Palmer, "The Debt-Bomb Crisis," reprinted in *Best of Business*, Spring 1983, p.91.

22. Cavanagh and Clairmonte, *op. cit.*, p.25; and calculations of the authors. On bank speculation, also see Michael Moffitt, *The World's Money* (New York: Simon and Schuster, 1983).

23. *New York Times*, December 3, 1984.

24. World Council of Churches, Advisory Group on Economic Matters of the Commission on the Churches' Participation in Development, *The International Financial System: An Ecumenical Critique* (Geneva, 1985), p.24.

25. Jeff Frieden, "On Borrowed Time," *NACLA Report on the Americas*, Vol. XIX, No. 2, March/April 1985. See also "International finance and state capitalism in Mexico, Brazil, Algeria, and South Korea," *International Organization*, Vol. 35, No. 3, Summer 1981.

26. For a critical study of Brazil's "economic miracle," see Celso Furtado, *No to Recession and Unemployment* (London: Third World Foundation, 1984).

27. Ruth Leger Sivard, *World Military and Social Expenditures, 1983* (Washington, D.C.: World Priorities, 1984), p.24. Calculated at 1979 constant prices, military expenditures in Third World countries amounted to $33 billion in 1972. Ten years later, in 1982, the figure had reached $131 billion. Stockholm Interna-

tional Peace Research Institute, *SIPRI Yearbook* (London, 1982), p.140.

28. For an excellent overview of the Third World arms industry, see Michael Klare, *America's Arms Supermarket* (Austin: University of Texas Press, 1984); also see Geoffrey Aronson, "The Third World's Booming New Industry: Weapons," *Washington Post,* June 16, 1985.

29. The most thorough accounting of Philippine capital flight was done in a three part series by Pete Carey, Katherine Ellison and Lewis Simons, in *The San Jose Mercury News,* June 23-25, 1985. See also John Lind, *Philippine Debt to Foreign Banks* (San Francisco: Northern California Interfaith Committee on Corporate Responsibility, November 1984), p.15.

30. *San Jose Mercury, op. cit.,* June 23, 1985, p.1.

31. *Journal of Commerce,* August 6, 1984.

32. Larry Sjaastad, "Where the Latin American Loans Went," *Fortune,* November 26, 1984. For a detailed account of the role of banks in capital flight, see Penny Lernoux, *In Banks We Trust* (New York: Doubleday, 1984). Western bankers estimate that as much as $100 billion of new loans was recycled back from Latin America to the United States and Western Europe in 1981-1982 by private businesses who evaded foreign exchange controls. *The Economist,* April 30, 1985, p.18.

33. Chris Edwards, *The Fragmented World* (New York: Methuen, 1985), p.173.

34. The Brandt Commission, *Common Crisis, North-South: Cooperation for World Recovery* (Cambridge, MA: MIT Press, 1983), p.74.

35. Overseas Development Council, *U.S. Foreign Policy and the Third World: Agenda 1982* (Washington, D.C., 1982), p.244.

36. World Bank, *World Development Report, 1983* (Washington, D.C., 1983), p.45.

37. World Bank, *World Debt Tables, 1983* (Washington, D.C., 1983).

38. D. Sykes Wilford, "What Went Wrong with LDC Finance?" *Euromoney,* May 1985, p.220.

39. See Michael Moffitt, "Economic Decline, Reagan Style," *World Policy Journal,* Summer 1985; and Michael Mussa, "U.S. Macroeconomic Policy and Third World Debt," unpublished manuscript, January 1984.

40. Quoted in *SANE World,* March 1985.

41. Pedro-Pablo Kuczynski, "Latin American Debt: Act Two," *Foreign Affairs,* Fall 1983.

42. *The Economist,* October 16, 1982, p.16.

43. Morgan Guaranty Trust, *World Financial Markets,* May 1982, p.8.

44. *Ibid.,* February 1983, p.5.

45. Evans, *op. cit.,* p.118.

46. *South,* July 1983, p.63. Real dollar interest rates (nominal rates adjusted for inflation in the U.S.) reached a historic high of

7.2 percent in 1984, compared with the recent peak of 6.9 percent in 1982. See World Bank, "Coping With External Debt in the 1980s," background document for the Development Committee meeting of April 18-19, 1985 (Washington, D.C., February 27, 1985), p.9.

47. *Institutional Investor*, May 1985, p.87.
48. *Ibid.*, p.88.
49. IMF, *World Economic Outlook* (Washington, D.C., 1981), p.124.
50. Castro, *op. cit.*, p.62., Still, in 1985, a gallon of petroleum at the gas station cost less than a gallon of Perrier water.

Chapter 3

1. The United States has systematically opposed loans to Nicaragua through the World Bank and Inter-American Development Bank, despite that country's excellent record in implementing loan projects. The U.S. motivation is clearly political. See Peter Kornbluh, *Nicaragua: The Price of Intervention* (Washington, D.C.: Institute for Policy Studies, 1985).

2. For a history of how the IMF and World Bank gradually adopted a strong export-oriented ideology, see Robin Broad, *op. cit;* and Walden Bello et al., *Development Debacle: The World Bank in the Philippines* (San Francisco: Institute for Food and Development Policy, 1982).

3. William Cline, *International Debt and the Stability of the World Economy* (Washington, D.C.: Institute for International Economics, 1983), p. 71.

4. For an elaboration of the U.S. position on debt, see the address of Ambassador William Middendorf, U.S. Permanent Representative to the Organization of American States before the International Conference on Latin America sponsored by the Center for International Relations, San Jose, Costa Rica, February 22, 1985, available from the State Department. For the World Bank's view, see World Bank, "Coping With External Debt in the 1980s," *op. cit.*

5. Financial Panel of the Economic Policy Council of the United Nations Association of the USA, Inc., *The Global Repercussions of U.S. Monetary and Fiscal Policy* (New York, 1984), p.38. For detailed analyses of private banks and debt policy, see Richard Feinberg and Valeriana Kallab, eds., *Uncertain Future: Commercial Banks and the Third World* (Washington, D.C.: Overseas Development Council/Transaction Books, 1984); and Fred Bergsten et. al., *Bank Lending to Developing Countries: The Policy Alternatives* (Washington, D.C.: Institute for International Economics, April 1985).

6. For an extensive listing of such proposals, see International Reports, Inc., *The A to Z of Debt Relief Schemes* (New York, 1985).

7. The Brandt Commission, *North-South: A Programme for Survival* (Cambridge, MA: MIT Press, 1982); see also The Brandt Commission, *Common Crisis, North-South: Co-operation for World Recovery* (Cambridge, MA: MIT Press, 1983).

8. For details of the plan, see *The A to Z of Debt Relief Schemes, op. cit.*, pp. 19-20; and Felix Rohatyn, "A Plan for Stretching Out Global Debt," *Business Week*, February 28, 1983.

9. Peter Kenen, "Third World Debt: Sharing the Burden, A Bailout Plan for the Banks," *New York Times*, March 6, 1983. Kissinger proposes the establishment of a Western Hemisphere Development Institution, financed by the industrial governments, to lend at low interest rates to developing countries. See *Washington Post*, June 25, 1985.

10. James Weaver and Howard Wachtel, "The LDCs, the IMF,

AID and the link between them," (Washington, D.C.: American University, 1984), p. 39.

11. The leading African spokesperson on debt has been President Julius Nyerere of Tanzania. As chairman of the Organization of African Unity in 1984, Nyerere stated: "Third World countries have the power of debt. . . . They should simply refuse to pay." *International Herald Tribune*, November 17-18, 1984. See also, interview with Nyerere in *South*, August 1984; and the lengthy section on the IMF in Africa in *South*, July 1985.

12. Among others, the Socialist International and the Latin American Parliament proposed in 1985 that a ceiling of 20 percent of export earnings be set on debt service.

13. This includes ministers from Colombia, Argentina, Brazil, Mexico, Venezuela, Peru, Bolivia, Chile, Uruguay, Ecuador and the Dominican Republic. See *Washington Post*, June 22, 1984.

14. *Institutional Investor*, July 1984, p. 94.

15. *Ibid.*

16. The background papers and resolutions of the South-North Conference on "The International Monetary System and the New International Order" were published in *Development Dialogue* (Uppsala, Sweden), No. 2, 1980.

17. World Council of Churches, Advisory Group on Economic Matters of the Commission on the Churches' Participation in Development, *op. cit.*

18. Intergovernmental Group of Twenty-four on International Monetary Affairs, "Report on the Task Force on the Reform of the International Monetary and Financial System," Washington, D.C., September 2, 1983.

19. See Cheryl Payer, *The Debt Trap: The International Monetary Fund and the Third World* (New York: Monthly Review Press, 1974); Teresa Hayter, *Aid as Imperialism* (Harmondsworth: Penguin, 1971); and "The Position of the Greens in the West German Parliament regarding the International Debt Crisis, the IMF, and World Bank Policy," unpublished statement of September 25, 1984.

20. Latin America Bureau, *The Poverty Brokers: the IMF in Latin America* (London: Latin America Bureau, 1983), p.116.

21. *Ibid.*, Chapter 7.

22. United Nations General Assembly Resolution 3201 (S-VI), *Declaration and Action Programme on the Establishment of a New International Economic Order* (New York: United Nations, May 1, 1974).

23. United Nations Conference on Trade and Development, *The Least Developed Countries*, TD/B/1027 (New York, 1984).

24. For a discussion of bank reaction to debt forgiveness proposals, see Bergsten, et al., *op. cit.*, pp. 192-194.

25. *Congressional Record*, September 23, 1980, pp. S13202-S13203. For a similar approach, see Tony Killick, et. al., "The IMF: Case for a Change in Emphasis," in Richard Feinberg and Valeriana Kallab, eds., *Adjustment Crisis in the Third World*

(Washington, D.C.: Overseas Development Council/Transaction Books, 1984).

26. In 1985, Fidel Castro became a leading Third World spokesperson advocating the cancellation of "illegitimate" debt. See Fidel Castro, *On Latin America's Unpayable Debt, Its Unforeseeable Consequences and Other Topics of Political and Historical Interest* (Havana: Editora Politica, 1985); and Arthur Schlesinger Jr., "Castro on the Debt Crisis," *Wall Street Journal*, June 12, 1985.

27. Valuable work on participatory development and alternative aid policies in the United States is being carried out by the Washington D.C.-based Development Group for Alternative Policies (1010 Vermont Ave., NW, #521/Washington, D.C. 20005). For an excellent overview (and an extensive bibliography on development literature), see Guy Gran, *Development By People* (New York: Praeger, 1983). See also, Michael Watts, *Silent Violence: Food, Famine, and Peasantry in Northern Nigeria* (Berkeley: University of California Press, 1984); Stephen Bunker, *op. cit.*; and A.F. Robertson, *People and the State: An Anthropology of Planned Development* (Cambridge University Press, 1984). Useful publications include: *IFDA Dossier* (Nyon, Switzerland), *Rural Development Abstracts,* and the monthly review column in *World Development.*

28. For an overview of the Congressional debate on the AID/IMF linkage, see "Kemp Moves to Sever Linkage of Economic Aid to IMF Rules," *Congressional Quarterly,* June 23, 1984, p. 1503.

29. Charles Schumer and Alfred Watkins, "Faustian Finance," *The New Republic,* March 11, 1985.

30. *Ibid.,* p. 15.

31. On July 5, 1985, IMF managing director Jacques de Larosiere referred to U.S. dependence on $100 billion a year of capital inflows to service its debt as a process which "cannot continue indefinitely." Larosiere claimed that the United States was importing one-sixth of the net savings of the rest of the world. From speech to the Economic and Social Council of the United Nations in Geneva, quoted in *Financial Times,* July 6, 1985.

32. Don Pease and William Goold, "The New GSP: Fair Trade with the Third World," *World Policy Journal,* Spring 1985.

33. *Far Eastern Economic Review,* February 7, 1985.

34. For a comprehensive national program for the farm crisis, see *Beyond Crisis: Farm and Food Policy for Tomorrow* (Washington, D.C.: Rural Coalition, December 1984).

35. See Susan George, *Ill Fares the Land* (Washington, D.C.: Institute for Policy Studies, 1985). For an excellent overview of debt and the family farm, see Shantilal Bhagat, *The Family Farm: Can it be Saved?* (Elgin, IL: Brethren Press, 1985), pp. 46-50.

APPENDICES

Appendix I
African Debt: A New Initiative

It might be called the forgotten debt. Invisible on the financial pages of the Western press, African debt has nonetheless grown to catastrophic proportions for the populations of much of the continent. Indifference towards Africa's external debt in the West is rooted in simple figures: only one of every seven dollars owed by Third World nations is held by Africans. There are no Mexico's or Brazil's on the continent, no single country that could threaten the international banking system with a default.

Yet, the debt service to export earning ratios of most African nations are higher than those of their neighbors in Latin America. And, at any given moment over the last 4 years, over half of the International Monetary Fund's austerity programs were in effect in African nations. This indebtedness is crushing all possibilities for development by diverting scarce foreign exchange and sizable local resources toward debt repayment. In sub-Saharan Africa, the resource squeeze has been exacerbated by the worst drought of the last century, one which threatens to dispossess millions of small producers from their land and further damage the environment.

While the debt is currently a major burden, it can also be viewed as a challenge. Avenues exist to transform much of this debt into development. Most African debt is owed to government sources in the West. Hence, citizens groups can exert a far greater influence on what to do with the debt than they can toward Latin American debt, most of which is owed to private banks. Certain Western nations have already cancelled some of the debt owed to their governments. Members of the Debt Crisis Network have been exploring the means to shift debt payments to the U.S. government into local development funds. Part of the problem (and hence the seeds of a more just resolution) rests in development strategies pursued by African nations over the past two decades.

The Road to Debt Peonage

Since the 1970s, many African countries have suffered stagnation in peasant agriculture and deterioration in their balance of payments. This stagnation cannot be understood in isolation from the strategies of export-led development promoted by bilateral and multilateral donors, most notably the World Bank and IMF. Also as a result of pursuing such strategies, the external debts of African nations soared.

Soon after independence, many African countries embarked on development strategies which combined both export promotion of primary products and (in the more developed countries) import-substitution industrialization. Both were largely dependent on Western financial and technological inputs. While serving local elites and Western interests in the short-term, this approach widened inequalities and ultimately bankrupted economies. In countries with limited resources, the spread of export crops usurped land once devoted to staple food crops. As lands were opened to more capital-intensive cash crop plantations, peasants were dislocated from rural areas into urban slums.

Africa's economic difficulties spilled out into the open in the early 1980s as real growth lost pace to soaring external debts, and per capita domestic product began to decline. Principal factors contributing to stagnation included a high priced, import-intensive industrial sector; low world prices for the region's export commodities; and bottlenecks in the agricultural sector. Chronic trade and balance of payments deficits required additional borrowing and the debt spiral continued.

The Debt Grows

According to a 1985 survey by the Economic Commission for Africa/Organization of African Unity, the total external debt of 45 African countries grew from a low of $10.6 billion in 1971 to $137 billion by the end of 1984, an average annual growth rate of 25 percent (see Table 1). If short-term debt (maturity of less than one year) is added to the 1984 total, the figure jumps as high as $175 billion.

Lending by both official and private sources accounted for the rapid growth, with the latter increasing its share from 33 to 40 percent of the total between 1971 and 1983. Growth of private loans was particularly rapid during the 1970s, after which the onset of economic stagnation across Africa deterred commercial bank lending.

As debt grew, debt service payments grew faster, from $1 to $15 billion over the 12 year span. Reflecting the higher interest

TABLE 1
External Debt of 45 African Countries
($ billion)

	1971	1975	1978	1979	1980	1983
Debt Outstanding	10.6	25.7	89.5	108.4	118.4	133.8
Official	7.1	15.7	49.5	58.1	67.2	80.2
Private	3.5	10.1	40.0	50.3	51.2	53.6
Principal Payments	0.7	1.7	3.4	4.5	6.5	9.8
Official	0.3	0.6	0.7	1.0	1.2	2.1
Private	0.4	1.1	2.7	3.5	5.3	7.7
Interest Payments	0.2	0.8	2.1	3.2	4.3	4.9
Official	0.1	0.3	0.9	0.9	1.2	1.6
Private	0.1	0.5	1.2	2.3	3.1	3.3
Total Debt Service	1.0	2.5	5.5	7.8	10.9	14.8
Official	0.5	0.9	1.7	1.9	2.4	3.7
Private	0.5	1.6	3.8	5.9	8.5	11.1
Net Transfers	0.9	5.7	10.6	8.5	5.8	3.2
Official	0.6	2.7	3.9	4.6	5.1	3.7
Private	0.3	3.0	6.7	3.9	0.7	−0.3
Debt Service/exports*	9.6	N.A.	11.4	11.7	12.5	25.0
Debt/exports*	85.0	N.A.	116.8	104.7	90.3	121.2
Debt/GNP	16.3	18.4	28.2	28.8	26.1	36.0

*As a percent of exports of goods, services and private transfers.
Source: Economic Commission for Africa and Organization of African Unity.

rates and shorter repayment periods on private debt, its share jumped from 50 to 75 percent of total debt service. Debt service as a percent of export earnings rose from 10 to 25 percent, and as high as 100 percent for Tanzania, Sudan and Zambia.

A turning point for African development occurred in 1979 when the net transfer of finance (new loans minus debt service) into Africa began to decline. As private banks abandoned Africa, the net transfer dropped from over $10 billion in 1979 to $3 billion in 1983. Net transfers with private sources actually went negative in 1983, reflecting banks' retrenchment from lending for projects and their willingness to lend only enough to ensure that their previous loans could be serviced.

Part of the strain on African nations is seen in the hardening of the terms for lending. Average interest rates charged jumped from 5.6 percent in 1975 to as high as 10 percent in 1981; only in 1984 did they move back down to manageable levels of 5.8 percent. The average maturity as well as the share of concessional debt likewise fell quite sharply from 1975 to 1983, and only began to improve in 1984. The share of external finance that was on a grant basis also fell from 47 percent in 1970 to 30 percent in 1975 to 17 percent in 1983. While many of these indicators did ease up a bit in 1984, it was after half a decade of worsening terms and general economic stagnation. This slight improvement in terms in 1984 through the present also coincided with the period when the major IMF lending of 1981–83 had to be repaid. Many countries simply do not have the foreign exchange to stay even close to debt service schedules.

TABLE 2
Terms of lending for Sub-Saharan Africa (percent)

Average terms	1975	1978	1980	1982	1983	1984
Interest	5.6	6.6	7.3	7.9	8.1	5.8
Official	4.2	3.8	3.9	4.8	6.0	4.2
Private	8.3	9.4	11.2	11.1	10.9	10.4
Maturity (years)	19.9	16.5	17.5	18.5	15.9	23.6
Official	26.3	25.3	25.0	27.3	23.5	29.2
Private	8.4	8.0	8.7	9.1	6.1	8.0
Share of debt:						
Concessional	46.3	40.2	38.1	36.9	35.6	36.9
Variable int.	10.0	15.2	18.7	22.6	22.7	21.8
IMF credits ($bn)	0.6	1.3	2.0	4.0	5.1	5.3

Source: World Bank, World Debt Tables, 1985–86 Edition, Washington, D.C. 1986.

While external debt is crippling development efforts across the entire continent, one set of countries deserves special attention. According to figures of the Economic Commission for Africa, the poorest 29 African countries (with populations of over 1 million) have accumulated external debts of over $45 billion, debt on which the countries have been paying annual service payments of over $3 billion annually (see Table 3). Over

TABLE 3
Debt and Development in Africa's 29 Poorest Nations*

	GNP per capita ($) 1983	Debt per capita ($) 1983	External debt ($mn) 1983	of which official debt ($mn) 1983	Debt service payments ($mn) 1983	Debt service paid as % of exports 1982	Debt owed to US gov't ($mn) Sept., 1985
Ethiopia	120	40	1,326	1,201	80	9	114
Mali	160	129	905	889	12	6	5
Zaire	170	141	4,380	2,981	81	5	1,069
Burkina	180	76	453	417	17	14	n.a.
Malawi	210	65	755	539	56	23	35
Uganda	220	47	657	612	98	256	11
Burundi	240	81	324	316	18	5	n.a.
Niger	240	137	824	534	95	24	11
Tanzania	240	118	2,350	2,233	126	24	125
Somalia	240	254	1,269	1,189	27	24	202
Rwanda	270	39	233	233	6	3	1
Centr. Afr. Rep.	280	110	220	159	9	5	3
Togo	280	333	1,000	667	36	12	2
Benin	290	151	603	274	56	20	23
Guinea	300	223	1,335	1,135	80	16	99
Ghana	310	125	1,500	1,277	65	32	169
Madagascar	310	229	2,060	1,321	112	33	50
Sierra Leone	330	144	433	329	37	16	43
Kenya	340	164	2,950	1,932	376	27	236
Sudan	400	284	5,688	4,213	104	21	486
Chad	400	30	152	126	1	0	n.a.
Mozambique	400		n.a.	n.a.	n.a.	n.a.	52
Senegal	440	397	2,086	1,694	102	14	33
Lesotho	460	167	167	155	14	16	n.a.
Liberia	480	455	910	707	33	6	207
Mauritania	480	640	1,280	1,139	40	12	7
Zambia	580	672	4,030	2,916	184	17	282
Ivory Coast	710	631	5,680	1,682	997	34	95
Zimbabwe	740	243	1,940	439	146	15	38
Total			**45,504**	**31,309**	**3,008**		**3,398**

*with population of over 1 million

Source: Calculated by John Cavanagh and Fantu Cheru from statistics of the World Bank, Economic Commission for Africa, and the United States government.

two-thirds of this is official debt, spread across dozens of creditor governments and multilateral banks. Hence, Western governments have tremendous room to act as overall exposure for each of them is small.

Toward a More Rational Approach

In 1981, the United Nations Conference on Trade and Development (UNCTAD) called for the conversion of all outstanding bilateral governmental loans into grants for the 36 least developed countries in the world. Already, several governments have cancelled a total of $2.8 billion in debt to these countries: West Germany—$1.7 billion; United Kingdom—$227 million; Canada—$188 million; Netherlands—$157 million; and smaller amounts by France, Denmark, Sweden, Italy, Japan, Finland and Switzerland.

Thus far, the United States is visibly absent. Of the $45 billion in external debt owed by the 29 poorest nations in Africa (with populations of over 1 million), $3.4 billion is owed to the U.S. government. The money owed to the U.S. government falls into four categories:

Development/economic assistance	$842 million
PL 480 (Food for Peace)	1,085 million
Military assistance	459 million
Export-Import Bank	1,012 million
TOTAL	$3,398 million

Legislative avenues exist to transform the first two categories of this debt (up to $2 billion) into development:

Development/Economic Assistance

In 1978, the Foreign Assistance Act of 1961 was amended to include Section 124 on "Relatively Least Developed Countries." This section provides that the President may waive both principal and interest on prior assistance for the 36 least developed countries (including 18 of the poorest 29 African nations). If such funds are waived, an equivalent amount of local currency is to be placed in a local currency account to be used for development activities consistent with the Foreign Assistance Act.

Were this section to be made mandatory ("the President *shall* waive...") and extended to the full 29 African nations, it would free up precious foreign exchange and channel much needed local currency into development projects. At present, there are hundreds of projects in Africa that are stagnating for lack of local currency. Health, education and nutrition projects, with high recurrent local currency costs to pay personnel, are particularly hard hit. Since this aid is highly concessional (2–3 percent interest and up to 30 year repayment periods), these 29 nations owe less than $50 million per year on the $842 million. This amount is small for the U.S., yet it could pay the salaries of many teachers and health care workers.

PL-480 (Food for Peace)

PL-480 provides concessional sales of U.S. agricultural goods to developing countries. Title III was added in 1977, which allows countries to reduce or eliminate their debt to the U.S. government under the program if they agree to use the proceeds from local sale of the PL-480 food to initiate agricultural or development projects.

Title III has been little used, apparently due to two strict conditions. First, countries have had a great deal of difficulty showing that the projects they would initiate are new, not ones the government was already planning. Second, tough macro-economic conditionality is attached. Once again, here is a large potential reservoir of development funds: over $1 billion for these 29 countries. Would it not make sense to eliminate these two conditions and transform the food debt into local currency accounts that could be devoted to environmentally sound development assistance?

One agency that could help oversee and manage the dispersal of local currency funds is the United Nations International Fund for Agricultural Development (IFAD). IFAD has a mandate to support efforts of small farmers to increase local food production throughout the Third World. It also has experience working with grassroots organizations and other indigenous non-governmental development groups in putting together projects that benefit the local population. IFAD has provided loans in Bangladesh, for example, to 84,000 landless peasants who previously relied on moneylenders that charged up to 100 percent interest. These peasants now earn their living through such diverse trades as weaving fishing nets and making jewelry. To encourage local organizations, the credit is routed through local banks to a small group of people who come together to obtain a loan.

In 1984, IFAD lent Ethiopia $1 million aimed at helping peasants to increase agricultural production. The money was chanelled through the National Agricultural and Industrial Development Bank, which had traditionally lent money only for cash crop production. The loans were used to finance food production for local consumption and served the needs of 375,000 peasants.

Managers of local currency funds should be encouraged to pursue innovative means to dispense resources. In particular, forms of reimbursement in kind should be encouraged. Governments could forgo a certain amount of local currency repayment by preserving their national heritage, through conservation or reforestation programs. The currency value of such programs could be determined through negotiation between creditor and debtor country.

These are but suggestions of innovative steps that should be explored. The moment is long overdue to transform Africa's unsustainable debt burden into development.

Appendix II
Baker, Bradley and the U.S. Debate on Debt

During the summer of 1986, several new voices entered the U.S. debate over international debt and substantially changed its parameters. Until that time, the notion that portions of the debt could or should never be repaid was taboo in government and bank circles. That taboo has now been erased. Faced with mounting evidence that the austerity approach to debt management was both stagnating the Third World and increasingly hurting U.S. farmers, business and the trade balance, a few bankers and government officials began to break ranks. Led by Senator Bill Bradley, they argued that some form of debt write-off was essential to growth in the Third World. While the debate largely skirted the issue of how to promote participatory development, it broke down the monopoly in the debt debate that Treasury Secretary James Baker had held since the preceding fall.

In October 1985, before an assembly of the world's richest and most powerful financiers, the Reagan Administration announced a shift in its approach to the debt crisis. The announcement at the annual meeting of the World Bank and International Monetary Fund (IMF) was an attempt to steal the limelight in the global debt debate from initiatives by Latin American leaders Fidel Castro of Cuba and Alan Garcia of Peru. From a policy of official *nonrecognition* that a crisis even existed, Treasury Secretary James Baker publicly *recognized the problem*, announcing with great fanfare what amounts to a *nonsolution*: the celebrated ''Baker Plan.''

In short, the plan is too little, too late, too austere, and too costly. It fails to address the roots of the debt crisis and the fundamental question of how the costs will be shared.

What is the Baker Plan?

The Baker Plan addresses the situation of 15 countries where the gap between debt service owed and ability to pay is greatest:

10 in Latin America, 3 in Africa and 2 in Asia. It proposes 3 remedies for these countries:

1. Private commercial banks are urged to extend $20 billion in new loans to these countries over the next 3 years.

2. Multilateral financial institutions are urged to extend an additional $9 billion in new loans to these countries, with a rising share from the World Bank.

3. In return for the new financing, the developing country recipients are to initiate domestic reforms to decrease government involvement in the economy, and to impose "market opening measures" encouraging direct foreign investment and liberalizing trade.

TABLE 1
The Baker 15, 1985

Country	Foreign Debt (in billions)	Interest (in billions)	Debt Service Ratio (percent)	Debt Owed to U.S. Banks (in billions)	Annual Growth Rate of GDP, 1980–1984
Brazil	$103.5	$11.8	46.1	$23.8	0.1
Mexico	$97.7	$10.0	46.1	$25.8	1.3
Argentina	$50.8	$5.1	62.2	$8.1	– 1.6
Venezuela	$32.6	$4.1	28.9	$10.6	– 1.8
Philippines	$27.4	$2.1	38.9	$5.5	0.8
Chile	$21.9	$2.1	56.8	$6.6	– 1.4
Yugoslavia	$20.0	$1.7	15.3	$2.4	0.6
Nigeria	$18.0	$1.8	13.3	$1.5	– 4.7
Morocco	$14.4	$1.0	41.7	$0.9	2.5
Peru	$13.9	$1.3	41.9	$2.1	– 0.7
Colombia	$13.9	$1.3	28.9	$2.6	1.8
Ecuador	$7.9	$0.7	25.0	$2.2	1.1
Ivory Coast	$6.3	$0.6	22.2	$0.5	– 2.3
Uruguay	$4.9	$0.5	62.5	$1.0	– 3.7
Bolivia	$4.2	$0.4	50.0	$0.2	– 4.7
Total	$434.7	$44.5	36.9	$93.8	– 0.3

*Principal and interest payments as percent of exports of goods and services.

Sources: *Fortune*, 23 December 1985, Chase Econometrics, *Forecasts and Analysis*, various issues; and World Bank.

In backing the Plan and hence the new loans, the U.S. government in effect agreed to begin a taxpayer bailout of the banks without consulting the taxpayers. The response in developing countries—among governments, opposition parties, and popular organizations—has been almost universally negative. The following arguments give a flavor as to why.

Too Little

Compare the $29 billion in new credits over 3 years proposed by Baker to the following figures:

In 1983, developing nations spent approximately $50 billion servicing their debts; in return, private banks sent in $20 billion and multilateral agencies another $15 billion. This adds up to a net drain of $15 billion from the developing world in one year alone, a figure that doubles (perhaps even triples) if one adds illegal capital flight. This net drain has grown in the past two years. Debtor countries paid about $88 billion in 1985 in interest payments alone, about $45 billion of which came from the "Baker 15."

The Baker proposal amounts only to $9.3 billion in new funds for the 15 countries each year, and hence does not come close to covering the gap, let alone financing growth. Indeed, all the Baker money will ensure is that private banks receive slightly more debt service payments.

In addition, the Baker Plan, in covering only 15 countries, completely bypasses dozens of countries across Africa and elsewhere whose overall debts are small compared to Brazil or Mexico but whose debt service burdens are enormous in the context of their ability to pay. Tens of thousands face starvation in these countries, which can ill afford to siphon scarce foreign exchange into exorbitant debt service payments.

Too Late

Since the explosion of the debt crisis in 1982, it is estimated that per capita income in Latin America has plummeted by 15 percent. Under the pressure of IMF austerity plans, these countries have slashed imports (and tens of thousands of U.S. jobs in the process) and crippled their own industrial infrastructure by starving their factories of replacement parts and raw materials. Migration into the U.S., particularly from Mexico, has increased. The devastation already wrecked by the crisis will take decades to repair. A massive debt rescheduling, not $9 billion per year, is required.

Too Austere

Baker billed his initiative the "Program for Sustained Growth" and managed to lead the press and public into believing that "growth and the World Bank" will be substituted for "austerity and the IMF." A careful reading shows that this is not the real Baker plan: granting of "Baker loans" has been made contingent upon a country's compliance with an IMF austerity program. The program generally involves cutting government expenditures, freezing wages, devaluing the currency and cutting imports. In effect, the programs demand the dismantling of fragile social security nets precisely when they are needed most. Hence, the Reagan administration claim that the Plan replaces austerity with growth is a cruel lie. Too little to advance growth, the Plan is based on the continuation of austerity.

Coupled to IMF austerity, the Baker Plan adds an additional twist. Countries must impose the Reaganomic emphasis on privatization on top of austerity. In essence, this involves: removing roadblocks to foreign investment, reducing the number of state companies, and dropping protection from domestic private enterprises. The purported intent is to stimulate growth through exports.

The architects of this plan conveniently ignore that it is precisely this sort of approach that generated a good deal of debt (and numerous riots) in the first place. Brazil, Mexico, South Korea and the other giant debtors built up their now unpayable debts in drives to create huge export-oriented enclaves, enclaves which left them victims to slumping prices and stagnating markets over which they have no control. It also left them ill-equipped to meet the essential requirements of the majority of their own populations.

Too Costly

The Baker Plan conveniently bypasses one of developing countries' most fundamental complaints: the exorbitant rates at which developing countries pay interest on their debts. Countries are expected to continue paying at the current historically high real interest rates, rates which effectively leave little foreign exchange for development. In the words of *Business Latin America*, "No mention is made of cutting interest costs or restructuring debt, for example. Moreover, by relying heavily on variable-rate bank loans as the source of new funds, the Baker Plan may only exacerbate an already precarious situation."[1]

Baker After One Year

As this appendix goes to press (August 1986), the Baker Plan enters its tenth month. Almost weekly, Treasury Department officials claim "progress" in speeches and testimony. In May 1986, for example, Baker testified before Congress that the World Bank had structural or sector loan negotiations underway with 13 of the Baker 15.[2]

Beneath the claims, however, there is little to show. In the fall of 1985, the administration tried rather desperately to enlist a major debtor as the first candidate for a "Baker loan." In November of that year, Treasury Assistant Secretary David Mulford and Fed Chairman Paul Volcker made separate treks to Argentina to discuss a possible package. Argentine President Alfonsin declined. Mexico, devastated by the twin blows of a major earthquake and the slashing of oil prices, made it clear that policy changes of the sort demanded by Baker were simply impossible.

By early 1986, in an attempt to revive enthusiasm in the Plan, Baker turned attention to five of the smallest debtors among the 15: Ecuador, Colombia, Uruguay, Cote d'Ivoire, and Morocco. Again, this was little more than a public relations stunt. Each was already deep in negotiations with the World Bank and undertaking policy reforms which reduced the state role in the economy. Ecuadorian President Leon Febres-Cordero was treated to a White House dinner in January, given two World Bank loans, and heralded as a Baker Plan success.(3) In Africa, new World Bank loans to Morocco have been signed with similar fanfare.(4)

Failure in Baker's agenda is also manifest in the dollar figures for new lending. While some World Bank money is flowing, it is unlikely to be available in the quantities requested. Congressional committees have made it quite clear that in the era of Gramm-Rudman, the multilateral banks will not receive increased outlays.(5) Indeed, the U.S. is not even meeting its present commitments.

Private banks, despite their early pledge of support for Baker, have turned to other outlets for loans and have lent at far below the Baker level.(6) Any increase in their participation rests on several conditions that remain to be hammered out. In return for putting up more money, the major creditor banks will ask for government guarantees for new loans, more co-financing from the World Bank, and an easing of the monitoring of their banks by the Comptroller of the Currency.

The Timing

Why did Baker move in 1985? In addition to its general appeal to the large banks, the promulgation of the Baker Plan at the 1985 meeting of the World Bank/IMF was calculated to derail an emerging Third World consensus behind an alternative approach. In late spring of that year, Fidel Castro had launched the first of several headline grabbing meetings highlighting the unpayability of the debt. And in July, Peruvian President Alan Garcia sent tremors through Washington and New York with the announcement that Peru would pay no more than 10 percent of its export earnings to service its debt. Meetings of the

Organization of African Unity, the United Nations Economic Commission for Latin America, the Group of 77 and the non-aligned Movement all highlighted debt as the central issue for joint concern.

The Baker Plan was aimed to steal the show from Castro, Garcia and other Third World leaders. In this respect, it achieved initial success. By mid-1986, however, largely domestic economic concerns began to shake up the debate. A study by the Joint Economic Committee of the Congress pointed out that the debt-induced cutback of Latin American imports of U.S. goods was crippling U.S. farmers, manufacturers and the trade balance.

At the same time, the big 9 money center banks were earning record profits.(7) Several studies focussed attention on growing capital flight and the role of international private banking facilities in the major banks whose job it is to facilitate that flight.(8) Morgan Guaranty estimates that between 1976 and 1982, 18 debtors (including 12 of the Baker 15) sent $198 billion abroad in capital flight (see Table 2). James Henry, former chief economist of McKinsey & Co., estimates that U.S. banks have captured $100–120 billion of the capital in their private banking divisions, 60–70 percent of which comes from Latin America. The realization that banks could weather substantial losses opened the space for certain politicians to say what so many in the Third World had been arguing for years: write off part of the debt.

In a speech at a June 1986 conference in Zurich, Switzerland, Senator Bill Bradley advocated a substantial write-off: 3 percent of the outstanding principal on the debt in each of the next 3 years, and a reduction in interest rates paid to service the debt by 3 percent. In exchange, developing countries would be asked to ease up on trade restrictions. By our calculations, this would reduce the debt service to export earnings ratio of the top 15 debtors from 37 to 25 percent in the first year.

Bradley's speech sparked substantial reaction. Bankers, Rep. Jack Kemp, World Bank President Barber Conable, and Fed Chairman Paul Volcker were quick to criticize the proposals.(9) On the other hand *Business Week*, the *New Republic*, and Jeane Kirkpatrick responded with varying degrees of support. (10) Congressman Charles Schumer and former Security Pacific vice-president offered variations on the theme, calling for a 30 percent write-off of the debt.(11)

We welcome the debate, but seek to broaden it. If we are going to write off substantial portions of Third World debt, why should we not do the same for U.S. farmers ravaged by a debt crisis of surprisingly similar proportions? Can this rethinking of debt be extended to the development strategies that countries

TABLE 2
Estimated Capital Flight, 1976–1985
($ billion, minus sign indicates outflow)

| | Net direct investment inflows | Change in gross external debt | Current account balance[a] | Change in selected gross foreign assets[b] | Capital flight[c] | | |
					Total	1976–82	1983–85
Argentina	4	42	− 15	− 4	− 26	− 27	1
Bolivia	0	3	− 2	− 0	− 1	− 1	0
Brazil	20	80	− 77	− 13	− 10	− 3	− 7
Chile	2	16	− 16	− 3	1	0	1
Colombia	2	10	− 11	− 2	0	0	0
Ecuador	1	7	− 5	− 1	− 2	− 1	− 1
Mexico	11	75	− 29	− 3	− 53	− 36	− 17
Peru	0	8	− 6	− 2	− 0	1	− 1
Uruguay	1	4	− 3	− 1	− 1	− 1	− 0
Venezuela	− 0	26	10	− 5	− 30	− 25	− 6
Subtotal	40	270	− 154	− 33	− 123	− 93	− 30
India	0	22	− 8	− 5	− 10	− 6	− 4
Indonesia	2	27	− 15	− 9	− 5	− 6	1
Korea	0	40	− 22	− 6	− 12	− 6	− 6
Malaysia	9	19	− 12	− 4	− 12	− 8	− 4
Nigeria	2	18	− 15	4	− 10	− 7	− 3
Philippines	1	23	− 16	1	− 9	− 7	− 2
South Africa	− 2	16	2	2	− 17	− 13	− 4
Thailand	2	17	− 17	− 1	− 0	1	− 1
Subtotal	14	181	− 102	− 18	− 75	− 52	− 23
Total for 18 countries	**54**	**451**	**− 256**	**− 51**	**− 198**	**− 145**	**− 53**

a Minus sign indicates deficit.

b Official reserve assets and other foreign assets of official monetary authorities plus foreign assets of commercial banks and certain other banking institutions. Minus sign indicates increase in foreign assets.

c Apparent change in other foreign assets (minus sign indicates increase) through residual capital flows measured as the counterpart of the sum of net direct investment inflows, change in gross external debt, current account balance, and change in selected gross foreign assets.

Source: Morgan Guaranty, World Financial Markets, March 1986.

will pursue? Is this not an ideal moment to challenge the World Bank and IMF strategies that have contributed to the debt build-up in the first place?

The urgency remains. Roberto Macedo, chairman of the economics department at the University of Sao Paulo reflected on the precipitous rise in underweight babies, infant mortality and malnutrition: "What kind of young people are we preparing for the future, for the labor force and for citizens?"(12)

The debt crisis will be resolved. On whose shoulders it will be resolved is perhaps the most pressing question across the Third World today.

(1) *Business Latin America*, 11 December 1986.

(2) Statement by James Baker, Secretary of the Treasury before the Committee on Foreign Relations, United States Senate, May 20, 1986, p. 7.

(3) *Wall Street Journal*, 23 January 1986. Febres-Cordero did mention to U.S. officials his concern over graffiti in Quito which read: "Baker Plan—No!"

(4) The *New York Times* (5 May 1986) reported from Meknes, Morroco: "Ahmed, a ragged youth who pushes a wheelbarrow on a building site here, has never heard of James A. Baker 3d. But in his own way he is involved in a project that symbolizes the Treasury Secretary's proposed strategy for easing the debt burden in developing nations...."

(5) See *Washington Post*, 13 March 1986.

(6) See *New York Times*, 16 December 1985, and *Washington Post*, 17 May 1986.

(7) "The Impact of the Latin American Debt Crisis on the U.S. Economy," A staff study by the Joint Economic Committee of Congress, May 10, 1986.

(8) Morgan Guaranty, *World Financial Markets*, March 1986; and James Henry, "Where the Money Went?" *New Republic*, April 14, 1986.

(9) See William Cline, "Bradley's Debt Plan Won't Work," *Washington Post*, July 15, 1986; and *Washington Post*, July 22, 1986.

(10) *Business Week*, 28 July 1986; *New Republic*, July 28, 1986; and Jeane Kirkpatrick, "Consider the Bradley Plan," *Washington Post*, 21 July 1986.

(11) Testimony of Robert M. Lorenz, senior vice president of Security Pacific Bank, before the Joint Economic Committee of Congress, June 18, 1986.

(12) *Wall Street Journal*, June 12, 1986.

GLOSSARY

Amortization: Repayment of the principal of a loan spread out over a period of years.

Balance of Payments Deficit/Surplus: A country is said to have a balance of payments deficit when its income (credits from exports, cash inflows, loans, etc.) is less than its payments (debits such as imports, cash outflows, debt repayments, etc.). A balance of payments surplus occurs when income is greater than payments.

Capital Goods: Heavy industrial products used primarily in the production of other goods. Foundry equipment, machine tools and electric turbines are capital goods; shoes and radios are consumer goods.

Central Bank: The "bankers' bank," the central government authority charged with managing a nation's currency, protecting its value and regulating the growth of the money supply. The Federal Reserve System ("The Fed") is the central bank of the United States.

Debt Repudiation (also known as *Default*): The refusal to recognize a debt obligation. In the case of private firms, this usually leads to bankruptcy. In the case of a state, the debtor would likely have all its external assets seized and trade would probably be reduced to a barter system. Depending on the size of the repudiation, there could be profound destabilizing ramifications for both the national and international banking systems.

Debt Service Ratio: The ratio of debt service payments (i.e., interest plus principal payments) to a nation's exports. A debt service ratio below 20%, indicating that one-fifth of export earnings are going to service the debt, is generally considered manageable.

Devaluation: The reduction of a currency's value in relation to another currency or currencies. A devaluation can either be consciously implemented by governments or the unconscious result of trends in international currency markets.

Equity Capital: The value of the stockholders' investment. When a bank cannot collect its outstanding loans, the stockholders' equity bears the loss. This ensures that stockholders, rather than depositors or the Federal Deposit Insurance Corporation (FDIC), will absorb the initial losses on a bank's loan portfolio. When the value of bad loans exceeds the bank's equity capital, the bank is declared insolvent and closed by federal regulators.

Eurodollars: Eurodollars are claims on U.S. dollars held by banks, businesses and individuals outside of the United States. The market for Eurodollars dates from 1957 and grew rapidly during the 1960s and some of the 1970s. The Euromarket has become one of the largest international markets for short-term funds. In addition to the U.S. dollars, it also deals in other hard currencies.

Exposure: The amount of loans that any lender has outstanding to a given borrower.

Grace Period: The number of years before capital repayments (amortization) begin.

Hard Currency: Widely used in international trade and thus acceptable as a payment for imports or debt service; can be freely converted to other currencies. While there are no official designations, the currencies of the strong developed countries – the dollar, mark, yen, Swiss franc, British pound – are generally considered "hard."

IMF Quota: Amount of money paid by a nation into the IMF which determines both its voting power and the amounts of money it can draw from the IMF.

LIBOR (London Inter-Bank Offer Rate): The inter-bank lending rate in the Eurodollar market used as a reference point for floating rate loans. In recent years, the U.S. prime lending rate has been used instead. The borrowers prefer the LIBOR since it is at market rate. Banks prefer the U.S. prime rate since its is predetermined.

Liquidity: Generally, the degree to which an asset can be readily exchanged for cash money. A nation's (or a firm's) liquidity is the degree to which it is able to cover its current liabilities with current assets.

Moratorium: When a country suspends payments, but declares itself willing to continue some time in the future.

Paris Club: The Paris Club is the forum within which debtor countries negotiate the restructuring of public sector debt with their main creditor governments; the debts restructured in this forum consist of loans from the creditor governments and private export credits, guaranteed or insured by export credit agencies in the creditor countries.

Protectionism: The name given to a variety of government policies used to protect domestic industries from more competitive foreign competition. Protectionism primarily refers to tariffs or quota limitations on imports. It also encompasses subsidies on the production of domestic goods, multiple exchange rates and other protective mechanisms. Such so-called "non-tariff" policies have been used with increasing regularity in the past ten years, especially in the textile, garment and steel industries.

Refinancing of Debt: Part of the debt rescheduling process, it refers to new loans granted to the country specifically for its debt repayment obligations. (In essence, the banks are paying themselves, but adding the interest charges to the debtor's tab.)

Reschedule: To revise or postpone dates on which capital repayments are supposed to be made. Interest payments are rarely if ever rescheduled. Nicaragua is the only country in recent years to have obtained an interest payment rescheduling.

Special Drawing Rights (SDRs): Created in 1969, the SDR has become the IMF's offical unit of account. Its value is determined by reference to a basket of currencies. It is sometimes used as an accounting unit for transactions between governments and by some other international financial institutions.

Spread: The difference between the rate a bank pays when it borrows money and the interest rate it charges when the money is lent out.

Terms of Trade: The rate at which a country's exports can be exchanged for imports. When a country's terms of trade decline, as is the case of many developing countries, it is necessary to export more in order to import the same quantity of goods and services.

Trade Credits: Short-term loans granted either by banks, industrial corporations or government agencies to finance the purchase of specific goods.

Note: Certain entries for the glossary were taken from: NACLA, "Debt: Latin America Hangs in the Balance," *NACLA Report on the Americas*, Vol. XIX, No. 2, March/April 1985; and United Nations Non-Governmental Liaison Service, "Development in the Debt Trap," *Action Notes*, September 1984.